Praise for Stories from a Corporate Coach

'Stories from a Corporate Coach' is a great blend of old favourites and rich new material for group work. A valuable part of any coach's toolbox.
— Andrew Halfacre, coach, trainer and author of *First Know What you Want*

I often use stories to illustrate a point or to use a metaphor with clients. This is an excellent collection. They are short and easy to review so you can quickly choose the best one for the occasion. Thanks of compiling them Richard. - David Klaasen

Richard Winfield is an excellent writer. His 'Stories from a Corporate Coach' is a very useful book for trainers as well as coaches. It's full of wisdom. I'm a trainer and after completing the book I've come away with a couple of brilliant little gems for my training courses. Everyone responds to stories. Story telling is one of the best ways to change a theory into experience. I can't wait to use these stories in my new course as well as some of my 'tried and true' courses. - Beverly Taylor

Stories from a Corporate Coach

Telling stories is the oldest form of teaching ...

Richard Winfield

Editor *CorporateCoach*

Brefi Press

www.brefipress.com

Cover design by Chris Walker, Expressive Design.

First published in 2013 by Brefi Press

ISBN 978- 0-948537-07-3

www.brefipress.com

Acknowledgements

Who do I acknowledge for the gift of these stories?

For so many of them appear to have come out of the ether; they have been absorbed from teachers, radio programmes, books and newsletters ...

I have been fortunate to have been exposed to so many different sources; and, obviously, these seeds have taken root in the back of my mind ready to pop up from my subconscious when I started looking.

I started with 37 stories from back issues of *CorporateCoach* and then the number grew and grew as more memories and leads just started to appear. My first acknowledgement is to the Internet, that amazing - and new - resource and source of knowledge that has allowed me to put flesh on vague memories and even discover a few stories that are new to me..

Over the years I have studied repeatedly with Sue Knight and Robert Dilts, who have introduced me to the range of NLP stories. Others who I can identify as the source of stories include Krishna Kumar in India, Damien Zikakis in the USA, Roger Hamilton in Bali and Michael Skirving in the UK.

Sources for some stories are recognised.

For the rest of you, please accept my gratitude and my apologies. By sharing, you have helped enrich the rest of us.

Books by Richard Winfield

The New Directors Handbook

The NED Directors Handbook

The AIM Directors Handbook

essential Checklists for Directors and Boards

CPD Guides to . . . (series)

Reflections of a Corporate Coach Vol. 1

Stories from a Corporate Coach

www.BrefiPress.com

About the author

Richard Winfield is the founder and principal consultant of the Brefi Group and head of the Director Development Centre. He is a strategy consultant, facilitator and scenario planner, providing transition coaching to directors, boards and partnerships and helping them develop strategy and build teams.

Richard has a natural talent for collecting, integrating and simplifying ideas and then communicating them to others. He is the guy you call when you need to bring structure and clarity to your thinking. He helps you identify core issues and make the complex simple, holding the space for you to create your own solutions.

Throughout his career he has been committed to community building and getting systems changed to make things better. He is passionate about setting people free to achieve their untapped potential and is continually analysing, simplifying and improving.

A long time student of all forms of executive coaching, Richard has developed both a proprietary course to prepare candidates for professional qualification as executive coaches and the unique Invisible Coaching® process to teach individuals how to think and act like a natural coach.

In the late 1960s Richard gained an honours degree in civil engineering and a master's degree in highways and transportation, followed by a ten-year career as a transportation planner, for which he won an international silver medal. Then in the early 1980s he gained a masters degree in management, followed by careers as a management consultant and publishing entrepreneur, combining interests in business and the impact of public policy.

Since 1990 he has focused on management development and, more recently, on director development and corporate governance.

In 2001 he launched the CorporateCoach newsletter, which has had 20,000 readers.

He launched the Director Development Centre in 2009, combining his interests in strategy and structure with the increasing demand for improved standards of corporate governance.

In 2010 he launched the ASEC School of Executive Coaching to design, license and deliver coach training in Africa, Asia and the Middle East, and in 2011 registered Invisible Coaching® as a proprietary coaching system for individuals.

Richard has extensive consulting experience in the UK, North America, Europe, South and West Africa, Baltic States, Arabian Gulf and South East Asia. He has been involved in business planning roles with companies in America, Europe, the Arabian Gulf and South Africa, including a two and a half year contract for National Power to carry out a full human resource skills analysis, implement a management training programme and introduce an effective management team structure. For three years he was responsible for developing the directors and senior managers of an international engineering group, reporting direct to the chief executive.

Richard is an explorer; he likes exciting new places, exciting new people and exciting new experiences. This is how he has accumulated his knowledge, his wisdom and his rich source of anecdotes.

He is addicted to learning and personal development; he has studied with thought leaders in North America, Europe and Asia, and reads widely.

As well as reading, he enjoys vegetable gardening, landscape gardening and pond building. He has been a farmer, worked as a cowboy and is now an established author.

For further information:
www.richardwinfield.com

Follow me:

www.corporatecoach.co.uk

Twitter.com/rwinfield

Twitter.com/ASECcoach

Twitter.com/directorcoach

Facebook.com/richard.winfield.brefi

Linkedin.com/in/richardwinfield

Preface

Every speaker, trainer and coach needs a fund of stories. As you gain experience you will build up a reserve of your own anecdotes, and mine can be found in *Reflections of a Corporate Coach*.

Fortunately there is a wealth of teaching stories stretching back to the Old Testament and Aesop's Fables, through Sufi stories to contemporary stories from NLP.

Stories from a Corporate Coach is a collection of 100 stories and more than 100 inspiring quotations designed to be used in a teaching context. Most, though not all, are stories that I have come across during my career. I have aimed to make them short so that you can easily adopt them and drop them into a talk or a coaching session; and I have deliberately not explained their meaning. They are for you to use as you wish.

Some of them you will have come across before in different forms. As a story teller, you can adapt and develop them as you wish.

In the Appendix I have included a few classic stories which you might find useful, a well as explanations behind some of the stories included in short form.

I do hope that you find this collection useful. I have had such fun remembering and researching them.

Richard Winfield
February 2013

CorporateCoach

Many of the stories in this book were originally published in the weekly e-newsletter *CorporateCoach*.

CorporateCoach is a weekly email newsletter for senior executives and teams in organisations interested in using coaching to improve corporate performance.

Written by Richard Winfield, it has been published since 2001 with an eclectic mix of thought provoking commentaries, inspiring stories, book recommendations and detailed lessons on how to apply a coaching or organisation development aid.

If you enjoy reading 'Stories from a Corporate Coach', then why not subscribe and receive a new article every week.

www.corporatecoach.co.uk

Contents

Stories from a Corporate Coach

ONE

A Brother like that

A man named Paul received a car from his brother as a Christmas present. On Christmas Eve when Paul came out of his office, a street urchin was walking around the shining new car admiring it. "Is this your car, Mister?" he asked.

Paul nodded. "My brother gave it to me for Christmas." The boy was astounded. "You mean your brother gave it to you and it didn't cost you nothing? Boy, I wish..." He hesitated.

Of course Paul knew what he was going to wish for. He was going to wish he had a brother like that. But what this lad said jarred Paul all the way down to his heels.

"I wish," the boy went on, "that I could be a brother like that."

Paul looked at the boy in astonishment, then impulsively he added, "Would you like to take a ride in my car?"

"Oh yes, I'd love that." After a short ride, the boy turned with his eyes aglow and said, "Mister, would you mind driving in front of my house?

Paul smiled a little. He thought he knew what the lad wanted. He wanted to show his neighbours that he could ride home in a big automobile. But Paul was wrong again. "Will you stop where those two steps are?" the boy asked.

He ran up the steps. Then in a little while Paul heard

him coming back, but he was not coming fast. He was carrying his little crippled brother. He sat him down on the bottom step, then sort of squeezed up against him and pointed to the car.

"There she is, Buddy, just like I told you upstairs. His brother gave it to him for Christmas and it didn't cost him a cent. And someday I'm gonna give you one just like it... and you can see for yourself all the pretty things in the Christmas windows that I've been trying to tell you about."

Paul got out and lifted the lad into the front seat of his car. The shining-eyed older brother climbed in beside him and the three of them began a memorable holiday ride.

That Christmas Eve, Paul learned what Jesus meant when he had said: "It's more blessed to give.

TWO

A Consulting view of the Hot Air Balloon tale

Andrew M. Lothian, Insights Group

A man in a hot air balloon realised he was lost. He reduced altitude and spotted a woman below.

He descended a bit more and shouted, "Excuse me, can you help me? I promised a friend I would meet him an hour ago, but I don't know where I am."

The woman below replied, "You are in a hot air balloon hovering approximately 30 feet above the ground. You are between 40 and 41 degrees north latitude and between 59 and 60 degrees west longitude."

"You must be an engineer," said the balloonist.

"I am," replied the woman, "but how did you know?"

"Well," answered the balloonist, "everything you told me is technically correct, but I have no idea what to make of your information, and the fact is that I am still lost. Frankly, you've been no help whatsoever."

The woman below responded, "And you, you must be in management consultancy."

"That's amazing, I am," replied the balloonist, "but how did you know?"

"Well," said the woman, "you don't know where you are or where you are going. You have risen to where you were due to an ability to generate a large quantity of hot air. Coming down to earth you need to find someone to talk to. You made a promise which you have no idea how to keep, and you expect people beneath you to solve your problems. The fact is you are in exactly the same position you were in before we met, but now, somehow, you are blaming me."

Andy Lothian is Chief Executive of The Insights Group

THREE

A fable of unburdening

From Chapter Eight, *The New Psycho-Cybernetics*, Maxwell Maltz

This is a story of an obviously weary traveller, walking down a dusty road, with a large boulder hoisted on one shoulder, a knapsack full of bricks on his back, a huge pumpkin precariously balanced on his head, and a nest a sturdy weeds and vines wound around his legs so that he could only take short, hobbling steps. As you might imagine this human packhorse was hobbling along, uncomfortably stooped over, his progress slow and tedious, his physical struggle great.

A person sitting by the roadside called his hello and asked, "Say, traveller, why do you burden yourself with that big, heavy rock on your shoulder?"

Incredibly, the traveller said:, "Hmm. You know, I never noticed just how heavy it was before and, until you mentioned it, I hadn't given much thought to my reasons for taking it with me." After a few moments pondering, the traveller set the boulder down, left it by the side of the road, and walked on, a bit straighter, a bit quicker.

A little further along, he encountered another by-stander who queried him about the knapsack full of bricks. "Hmm. I'm glad you made mention of it," said the traveller, "I really hadn't paid any attention to what was in the knapsack." He took out all the bricks, left them at the roadside, and walked on.

A little further along, a curious child playing by the road called out to him. "Hey mister, why do you have all those weeds wrapped around your legs?"

The traveller took out his pocket knife and sliced away the weeds.

One by one, the bystanders made the traveller aware of his needless old burdens. So, one by one, he accepted the new awareness, rejected the old burdens and abandoned them by the side of the road. Finally, he was a truly free man, and walked straight and tall like such a man.

Were his problems the boulder, the bricks, the weeds? No, not at all. The one problem was his lack of awareness of them.

FOUR

Alice and the Cheshire Cat

This is an incident from Lewis Carroll's Alice in Wonderland.

One day Alice came to a fork in the road and saw a Cheshire cat in a tree.

"Would you tell me, please, which way I ought to go from here?"

"That depends a good deal on where you want to get to," said the Cat.

"I don't much care where –." said Alice.

"Then it doesn't matter which way you go," said the Cat.

"– so long as I get SOMEWHERE," Alice added as an explanation.

"Oh, you're sure to do that," said the Cat, "if you only walk long enough."

FIVE

Alligator River

This story has been designed for use in a discussion about values. Who is the most reprehensible, and what kind of person would be the opposite?

"Once upon a time there was a woman named Abigail who was in love with a man named Gregory. Gregory lived on the shore of a river. Abigail lived on the opposite shore of the river. The river that separated the two lovers was teeming with man-eating alligators. Abigail wanted to cross the river to be with Gregory.

Unfortunately, the bridge had been washed away. So she went to ask Sinbad, a riverboat captain, to take her across. He said he would be glad to if she would consent to go to bed with him before he takes her across. She promptly refused and went to a friend named Ivan to explain her plight. Ivan did not want to be involved at all in the situation. Abigail felt her only alternative was to accept Sinbad's terms. Sinbad fulfilled his promise to Abigail and delivered her into the arms of Gregory.

"When she told Gregory about her amorous means of getting across the river, Gregory cast her aside with disdain. Heartsick and dejected, Abigail turned to Slug with her tale of woe. Slug, feeling compassion for Abigail, sought out Gregory and beat him brutally. Abigail was happy to see Gregory getting his due. As the sun sets, we hear Abigail laughing at Gregory."

SIX

Amazing story of a maize maze

This story was reported by Ed Batista

A few weeks ago a family became lost in a corn maze in Massachusetts and called 911 in a panic. Police rushed to the scene and found them, unharmed, just 25 feet from the entrance to the maze. A brief flurry of media coverage resulted, in which the family were generally portrayed as dimwits lacking common sense. But mocking these people obscures the fact that we've all had similar experiences; their predicament was just an unusually literal example of being trapped by a mental model.

Many commentators wondered why the family didn't simply walk through the corn to escape the maze. They could have easily pushed aside the cornstalks, headed for the exterior and rescued themselves. But they didn't think they were in a cornfield; they thought they were in a maze, and while their failure to recognise the difference says something about their crisis management skills, it also says something about the power of mental models. They couldn't simply walk through the corn, because that would involve walking through walls, and that's impossible.

We habitually view the world through a series of mental models that shape our understanding of our circumstances, our relationships and ourselves. And while these mental models are essential tools in allowing us to navigate through life, they can easily lead us astray. Philosopher Alford Korzybski said "A map is not the territory it represents," and a mental model is not the reality it seeks to depict. But we can easily mistake our mental models for reality and apply them inappropriately.

We construct our mental models out of the meaning we extract from experience, and there's inevitably a loss of fidelity as we focus on certain aspects of an experience (while ignoring others), interpret that data, and then conceptualise it as a general principle. And the gap that exists between our mental models and reality will continually increase over time unless we compel ourselves to test our assumptions, gather new data and update our models – which requires consistent effort.

Ed Batista – Leadership & Executive Coach at the Stanford Graduate School of Business

Animal picture book

A grandmother was reading a picture book with her grandson, who lived on a farm.

First picture.

> "What's that?"

> "It's a lion."

> "Very good."

Second picture.

> "What's that?"

> "It's a zebra."

> "That's right, very good."

Third picture.

> 'What's that?"

> "An elephant."

> "Very good."

Fourth picture.

"And here's an easy one, what's that?"

"I don't know."

"Come one, you know this one."

"No, I am not sure."

"Come on now."

"I think it might be a Charolais cross Simmental."

EIGHT

Ask the tea lady

A group of marketers were having a meeting to decide how to increase the sales of toothpaste.

There were many suggestions from their brainstorming and market analysis, but none really caught their imagination.

At about 11.00 the tea lady arrived with her trolley of drinks and snacks.

One of the group said, "We talk about thinking outside the box. Why don't we ask the tea lady for a suggestion?"

This they did and, quick as a flash, she replied "Why don't you increase the size of the hole?"

NINE

Bamboo story (1)

You prepare the soil, pick the right spot, then plant the Chinese Bamboo seed. You water it and wait. But you wait an entire year and nothing appears. No bud, no twig, nothing.

So you keep watering and protecting the area and taking care of the future plant, and you wait some more.

You wait another year and nothing still happens.

Okay, you are a persistent person not prone to giving up, so you keep on watering. You water, check the soil, start talking to the ground, maybe even click your heels in some kind of growing dance you read about in the National Geographic. Another year passes and still no sign of growth.

It has been three years. Should you give up? Someone told you that it might take a while to really see the fruits of your efforts, so you keep on keeping on. More water, more talk, more dancing. The neighbours are wondering. And another year passes. No tree.

You now make a decision. If there is no tree on this date one year from now you will stop watering. Period.

So you begin year number five with the same passion as day number one. You water, you wait. You keep watering and keep waiting. You water some more and then, could it be? Is it really?

Yep, there it is, something sticking out of the dirt. You come back the next day and WOW it has really grown! In fact you come back each day for about six weeks and finally the Chinese Bamboo tree stops growing - but it is over 80 feet tall! Yes, 80 feet in six weeks! Well, not really. It is 80 feet in five years.

TEN

Bamboo story (2)

Once upon a time there was a farmer who had two gardens. One was in the mountains and the other was in the plains. The farmer loved both gardens very much. But in particular he loved one tree in the mountain garden. This tree was a bamboo.

Bamboo was very tall and very beautiful. The farmer used to visit Bamboo every evening to admire and enjoy her beauty. When the farmer was visiting, Bamboo would always dance beautifully, which made the farmer even happier. The farmer loved Bamboo very much, much more than other trees.

It so happened that there was once a drought in the plains, and the lower garden started to dry. The drought was so severe that the plants started to die off. The farmer was desperate to find a way of watering this garden. There was plenty of water in the mountains, but he had no way of taking the water to the plains. Then the farmer remembered his friend Bamboo.

So the farmer went to Bamboo one evening and they started talking. "Bamboo," said the farmer, "I love you a great deal."

Bamboo was very happy. Dancing, she responded, "I too love you so much, master." The master was pleased.

"So, Bamboo," said the master, "I want to use you."

"I am ready, master," answered Bamboo.

"But there is one condition," the master went on. "In

order to use you, I must cut you down."

Bamboo was grieved and very disturbed. "Master," said Bamboo, "you say you love me. Why then do you want to destroy me?"

"Bamboo," the master said, "I don't want to destroy you, I want to use you. But in order for you to be usable to me, I must cut you. If you are not ready to be cut, I cannot use you."

Bamboo was most unhappy, because she feared the pain. But because she loved the master and trusted him, she decided to let the master go on. So the master took a hatchet and cut down Bamboo. It was very painful.

The master said, "Good, but there is some more work to do on you; I have to chop off your branches."

Bamboo complained even more. "Master, you want to kill me now." The master remained silent; and seeing that he was serious, Bamboo decided to submit. The master took his hatchet again and cleaned off the branches until Bamboo was very clean. Then he said, "This is really good, Bamboo, but there is still one last thing. I have to pop out your inside."

Bamboo was terrified. The last two steps had been painful enough, but to pop out her inside -- that was unthinkable. Bamboo struggled with this. But then the master said, "I cannot use you unless I pop out your inside." Seeing that the master was serious, Bamboo again submitted.

The master took an iron rod and popped out the inside until Bamboo was hollow. It was extremely painful. But Bamboo was now ready to be used.

The master used Bamboo as a pipe to connect his two gardens. Soon water started to flow from the mountain garden into the garden in the plains. The plants were revived. Seeing her usefulness, both Bamboo and the master were very happy. They ended up greater friends than before.

ELEVEN

Basic Training

Found stuck on the door of a refrigerator in a roadside restaurant in Jacksboro, Texas.

> If you open it, you close it
>
> If you turn it on, you turn it off
>
> If you unlock it, you lock it
>
> If you break it, you fix it
>
> If you can't fix it, you get someone who can
>
> If you borrow it, you return it
>
> If you use it, you take care of it
>
> If you make a mess, you clean it up
>
> If you move it, you put it back
>
> If you make a promise, you keep it
>
> If you don't know how it works, don't touch it
>
> If it doesn't concern you, don't mess with it.

TWELVE

Blind golfers

An engineer, a doctor and a lawyer were playing golf when they came up behind a group of men who were playing very erratically and thus very slowly.

As they got more frustrated with the ongoing delay they asked who these people were; after all, this was a very select golf club allowing only proficient golfers as members. They discovered that they were firemen who, some years ago, had fought a major fire at the clubhouse and been blinded. The club had offered them life membership as a form of compensation.

The trio started to discuss what the club could have done for these firemen without disrupting the use of the course.

The doctor explained various medical and surgical processes that might have been able to save the men's eyesight.

The lawyer suggested that they should have sued the insurance company for a mammoth compensation payment.

The engineer asked: "Why don't we just ask them to play at night?" – a win-win for all.

THIRTEEN

Broken Windows theory

The Broken Windows theory was reported in Malcolm Gladwell's The Tipping Point

Broken Windows was the brainchild of the criminologists James Q Wilson and George Kelling. Wilson and Kelling argued that crime is the inevitable result of disorder. If a window is broken and left unrepaired, people walking by will conclude that no on cares and no one is in charge. Soon, more windows will be broken, and the sense of anarchy will spread from the building to the street on which it faces, sending a signal that anything goes. In a city, relatively minor problems like graffiti, public disorder, and aggressive panhandling are all the equivalent of broken windows, invitations to more serious crimes.

In the mid 1980s the New York Transit Authority put the Broken Windows theory into practice. Until then they had not worried about graffiti, preferring to focus on the larger questions of crime and subway reliability. But the theory claimed that the graffiti was symbolic of the collapse of the system.

A new management structure was introduced with a precise set of goals and timetables aimed at cleaning the system line by line, train by train. If a car came in with graffiti, the graffiti had to be removed during the changeover or removed from service.

The graffiti clean up took from 1984 to 1990. Then

the second stage of reclamation of the subway began, with a crackdown on fare beating.

Serious crimes on the subway system were at an all-time high. But it was believed that, like graffiti, fare beating could be a signal, a small expression of disorder that invited much more serious crimes. Until then, the transit police had not thought it worth their time to pursue, because there was only $1.25 at stake for each individual incident, and there were plenty of more serious crimes happening down on the platform and on the trains.

The bonus was that one in seven of those arrested were found to have an outstanding warrant for a previous crime, and one in twenty was carrying a weapon of some sort. Arrests for misdemeanours, for the kind of minor offences that had gone unnoticed in the past, went up fivefold between 1990 and 1994.

When Rudolph Giuliani became mayor of New York in 1994, the Broken Windows theory was applied to the New York Police Department, with a crack down on quality of life crimes, including drunkenness, littering and public urination.

Crime in the city began to fall as quickly as it had in the subways, demonstrating that seemingly insignificant quality of life crimes were tipping points for violent crime.

FOURTEEN

Christopher Wren's redundant columns

Next to Market Cross House in Windsor is the Guildhall. The building was completed by Sir Christopher Wren in 1690.

Wren, the greatest English architect of his time, who designed St. Paul's Cathedral in London, the Sheldonian Theatre in Oxford, and founded The Royal Society, lived in a Thamesside luxury home in Windsor and conveniently commuted to London by boat.

Windsor Guildhall was started by another architect but completed by Wren after the original architect had died. On close inspection you can see that the central columns do not touch the ceiling and tradition has it that the councillors of the time thought it needed four large pillars to support it in addition to the large beams used by the architect. Wren said it didn't but, against Wren's wishes, they insisted on the columns in the interest of safety.

Wren put in the pillars — but he left the columns an inch short of the ceiling and hid the gap with a thin crust of mortar.

Wren's pillars have never supported the building.

Unfortunately, it appears that this is another myth. However, it makes a good story.

It's true that Windsor does have four non-supporting columns, but no one has ever managed to find any evidence at all of them causing a dispute between Wren and his employers. One theory is that they started out as supporting columns, but have settled over the centuries, leaving an unintended gap; another is that they are purely decorative.

FIFTEEN

Cooking a ham

A newly married wife was preparing for her first dinner party. She had decided to bake a ham.

Her still interested husband was watching her and asked her why the first thing she did was to cut off the end.

"Why," she replied, "that's how my mother did it."

He was still confused and suggested that she ask her mother why it was necessary.

This she duly did, and got this reply: "Why, that's how my mother did it."

Fortunately, her mother was still alive, so the next step was to ask Grannie.

At last, a logical explanation: "When I was first married after the War, we had only a small cooker and the oven was too small to take a whole ham. So I got into the habit of trimming the end before I started to cook it."

SIXTEEN

Could there be fish in your dreams?

This story is a favourite of Sue Knight's.

There was a psychotherapist who believed that many of the problems people brought to him were characterised by the existence of fish in their dreams.

One day a client came to him and was discussing the problems he had.

"Tell me," said the psychotherapist, "did you dream last night?"

"I might have done," replied the client.

"And tell me, in this dream was there a river?"

"I don't think so," replied the client.

"Well, was there any water, if not a river?"

"I guess there could have been."

"And was there a pool on the ground?"

"I couldn't be certain, but it's possible," the client replied.

"And in this pool could there have been a fish?"

"I can't rule out the possibility that there might have been a fish."

"Aha!" said the psychotherapist. "I knew it!"

SEVENTEEN

David and Goliath

One of the best known characters of the Bible is David, who as a lowly shepherd boy defeated the mighty Philistine warrior Goliath, and then grew up to be King David of Israel - and human ancestor of Jesus.

When the Israelites were at war with the Philistines, the two armies faced each other from opposite hills with the Valley of Elah between them. Every morning for forty days, the mighty Goliath, a Philistine giant over nine feet tall and wearing full armour would come out, mocking and challenging the Israelites for someone to volunteer to fight him. No-one did.

One day, David, who was then too young for the army, arrived with some deliveries for his older brothers. He heard Goliath and immediately volunteered to fight him.

After turning down an offer of the king's own armour, which was too big for him, David went down to the creek and selected five suitable stones for his sling. Dressed in his simple tunic, carrying his shepherd's staff, slingshot and his pouch full of stones, David approached Goliath. The giant cursed at him, hurling threats and insults.

As Goliath moved in for the kill, David reached into his bag and slung one of his stones at Goliath's head. Finding a hole in the armour, the stone sank into the giant's forehead and he fell face down on the ground.

David then took Goliath's sword, killed him and then cut off his head.

When the Philistine army saw their hero defeated they dropped everything and ran, with the now victorious Israelites in hot pursuit, chasing and killing them and plundering their camp.

EIGHTEEN

Elephant in the rock

This is a story told by the spiritual teacher, Eknath Easwaran.

In ancient India there lived a sculptor renowned for his life-sized statues of elephants. With trunks curled high, tusks thrust forward, thick legs trampling the earth, these carved beasts seemed to trumpet to the sky. One day, a king came to see these magnificent works and to commission statuary for his palace. Struck with wonder, he asked the sculptor, "What is the secret of your artistry?"

The sculptor quietly took his measure of the monarch and replied, "Great king, when, with the aid of many men, I quarry a gigantic piece of granite from the banks of the river, I have it set here in my courtyard. For a long time I do nothing but observe this block of stone and study it from every angle. I focus all my concentration on this task and won't allow anything or anybody to disturb me. At first, I see nothing but a huge and shapeless rock sitting there, meaningless, indifferent to my purposes, utterly out of place. It seems faintly resentful at having been dragged from its cool place by the rushing waters. Then, slowly, very slowly, I begin to notice something in the substance of the rock. I feel a presentiment . . . an outline, scarcely discernible, shows itself to me, though others, I suspect, would perceive nothing. I watch with an open eye and a joyous, eager heart. The outline grows stronger. Oh, yes, I can see it! An elephant is stirring in there!"

"Only then do I start to work. For days flowing into weeks, I use my chisel and mallet, always clinging to my sense of that outline, which grows ever stronger. How the big fellow strains! How he yearns to be out! How he wants to live! It seems so clear now, for I know the one thing I must do: with an utter singleness of purpose, I must chip away every last bit of stone that is not elephant. What then remains will be, must be, elephant."

NINETEEN

Failures as learning

Two case studies you can use.

Michael Jordan

Michael Jordan is considered one of the greatest basketball players of all time; in his brief bio on NBA.com he is described as 'single-handedly redefining the NBA superstar' and yet to get there he openly admits to failing more than most. In a famous ad campaign launched by 'Nike', Michael is quoted as saying he has:

- Lost almost 300 games (that's more games than many NBA players have court time in)

- Missed over 9000 shots at goal (again more shots than an average NBA player even takes)

- 26 times he was given the ball to take the game winning shot and MISSED

Jordan goes on to say the reason he has succeeded boils down to his constantly failing and using failure as motivation to shoot for success.

In other words Jordan viewed failures as stepping stones towards success; his shooting average was just below 50% so to score he would have to take two shots, one to fail the other to score.

Thomas Edison

Considered the greatest inventor of his time, Thomas Edison, was responsible for over 1,000 different patents, some refinements of previous inventions but many completely new ideas.

Edison is famous not only for his inventions but also his attitude on failure. In his mind failure was simply another stepping stone on the road to success.

Unlike Michael Jordan however, Edison's rate of success was significantly below Jordan's 50% average. But unlike the average person Edison continued to try and try again.

The famous story goes, Edison failed to refine the light bulb (one of the few creations he merely refined but did not invent) so many times it took him 10,000 attempts to perfect. However rather than accepting failure 9,999 times he is quoted as answering questions on his failures as rather: 'I have not failed. I have just found 9,999 ways that do not work'.

TWENTY

Financial Planning

From Louis James, Casey Research

Dan was a single guy living at home with his father and working in the family business.

When he found out he was going to inherit a fortune when his sickly father died, he decided he needed to find a wife with whom to share his fortune.

One evening, at an investment meeting, he spotted the most beautiful woman he had ever seen. Her natural beauty took his breath away.

"I may look like just an ordinary guy," he said to her, "but in just a few years, my father will die and I will inherit $200 million."

Impressed, the woman asked for his business card and three days later, she became his stepmother.

TWENTY ONE

Finding common ground

According to Roger Fry, co-author of Getting to Yes, before parties attempt to negotiate they should try to build rapport, check each other out. This can be as little as just shaking hands or eating together. In particular, they should try to get inside each other's heads and recognise the emotions on either side.

When Ronald Reagan met Mikhail Gorbachev in Geneva in 1985, they sat by a roaring fire while they exchanged ideas.

A border war between Peru and Ecuador was avoided when Fisher advised the president of Ecuador to sit on a sofa with the Peruvian president and look at a map with him.

Finding a common interest was key. Another story relates to an Israeli and Palestinian negotiation at Camp David in the USA. They made no progress for several days, until one complained about the quality of the American coffee. The other agreed; they recognised a common interest and the barriers fell away.

TWENTY TWO

Finding the treasure within

This is a story told by Eckhart Tolle in *The Power of Now.*

A beggar had been sitting by the side of the road for thirty years.

One day a stranger walked by.

"Spare some change?" mumbled the beggar.

"I have nothing to give you," said the stranger. Then he asked: "What's that you're sitting on?"

"Nothing, " replied the beggar. "Just an old box. I've been sitting on it for as long as I can remember.

"Ever look inside?," asked the stranger.

"No," said the beggar. "What's the point, there's nothing in there."

"Have a look inside," insisted the stranger. The beggar, reluctantly, managed to pry open the lid. With astonishment, disbelief, and elation, he saw that the box was filled with gold.

TWENTY THREE

Following the rules to the letter

Mark Shuttleworth was the second space tourist and the first African to go into space. When he flew to the International Space Station in April 2002, he was 28 years old, and an Internet billionaire, having founded Thawte and sold it to Verisign for $575 million.

Shuttleworth flew on the Russian Soyuz TM-34 mission as a space flight participant and spent eight days at the International Space Station participating in experiments related to AIDS and genome research. He returned to Earth on Soyuz TM-33 and has since had a career as a philanthropist and open source software entrepreneur.

Before his flight he undertook a year of training and preparation, including seven months in Star City, Russia. For the weightlessness training he had to fly south to the Black Sea where the cosmonauts would be taken on a series of parabolic flight manoeuvres to simulate zero gravity.

The flight south was in an ancient and very basic Russian transport plane. The cosmonauts' equipment included a minibus for use at their destination. Before they were allowed to take off, the foreign guests were required to sit in the minibus.

Why was this?

Apparently, there was a European Directive that European citizens must always wear seat belts when taking off or landing. The aircraft was not equipped with seat belts for passengers. However, there were, of course, seat belts in the minibus, so that's where they must sit.

TWENTY FOUR

Good luck, bad luck

A father and his son owned a farm. They did not have many animals, but they did own a horse. One day the horse ran away.

"How terrible, what bad luck," said the neighbours.

"Good luck, bad luck, who knows?" replied the farmer.

Several weeks later the horse returned, bringing with him four wild mares.

"What marvellous luck," said the neighbours.

"Good luck, bad luck, who knows?" replied the farmer.

The son began to learn to ride the wild horses, but one day he was thrown and broke his leg.

"What bad luck," said the neighbours.

"Good luck, bad luck, who knows?" replied the farmer.

The next week the army came to the village to take all the young men to war. The farmer's son was still disabled with his broken leg, so he was spared. "Good luck, bad luck, who knows?"

None of the young men came back alive. The son recovered, and two horses produced foals that were all sold for a good price.

The farmer went to visit his neighbours to console and to help them, since they had always shown him such solidarity. Whenever any of them complained, the farmer would say: "Good luck, bad luck, who knows?" If someone was overjoyed about something, he would ask: "Good luck, bad luck, who knows?"

And the people of the village came to understand that life has other meanings that go beyond mere appearance.

TWENTY FIVE

How rich are we?

Story contributed by Ngee Kee

One day a father and his rich family took their son on a trip to the country with the firm purpose to show him how poor people can be.

They spent a day and a night on the farm of a very poor family. When they got back from their trip, the father asked his son,

"How was the trip?" "Very good Dad!" "

Did you see how poor people can be?" the father asked.

"Yeah!"

"And what did you learn?"

The son answered, "I saw that we have a dog at home, and they have four.

We have a pool that reaches to the middle of the garden; they have a creek that has no end.

We have imported lamps in the garden; they have the stars.

Our patio reaches to the front yard; they have a whole horizon."

When the little boy was finished, his father was speechless.

His son added, "Thanks, Dad, for showing me how 'poor' we are!"

TWENTY SIX

How to avoid stress

A well known speaker was asked by a large corporation to deliver the keynote speech at their annual conference.

He asked them what they would like him to speak about. They told him that they were having an increasing problem of stress in the workplace. Could he, please, offer something that would address this.

When the day arrived he held the audience's attention with a wide range of anecdotes and stories, but the organisers could not detect any link to stress.

What was he up to? Had he misunderstood their requirements, or was he letting them down?

He entertained the company for 44 minutes. Then in the last minute he said, "And what about stress? Oh, yes. The answer is simple. Do less."

TWENTY SEVEN

Inspiring story of creative generosity

Two men, both seriously ill, occupied the same hospital room.

One man was allowed to sit up in his bed for an hour each afternoon to help drain the fluid from his lungs. His bed was next to the room's only window.

The other man had to spend all his time flat on his back.

The men talked for hours on end. They spoke of their wives and families, their homes, their jobs, their involvement in the military service, where they had been on vacation.

Every afternoon, when the man in the bed by the window could sit up, he would pass the time by describing to his roommate all the things he could see outside the window.

The man in the other bed began to live for those one hour periods where his world would be broadened and enlivened by all the activity and colour of the world outside.

The window overlooked a park with a lovely lake. Ducks and swans played on the water while children sailed their model boats. Young lovers walked arm in arm amidst flowers of every colour and a fine view of the city skyline could be seen in the distance.

As the man by the window described all this in

exquisite details, the man on the other side of the room would close his eyes and imagine this picturesque scene.

One warm afternoon, the man by the window described a parade passing by.

Although the other man could not hear the band, he could see it in his mind's eye as the gentleman by the window portrayed it with descriptive words.

Days, weeks and months passed.

One morning, the day nurse arrived to bring water for their baths only to find the lifeless body of the man by the window, who had died peacefully in his sleep. She was saddened and called the hospital attendants to take the body away.

As soon as it seemed appropriate, the other man asked if he could be moved next to the window. The nurse was happy to make the switch, and after making sure he was comfortable, she left him alone.

Slowly, painfully, he propped himself up on one elbow to take his first look at the real world outside. He strained to slowly turn to look out the window besides the bed.

It faced a blank wall.

The man asked the nurse what could have compelled his deceased roommate, who had described such wonderful things outside this window.

The nurse responded that the man was blind and could not even see the wall. She said, 'Perhaps he just wanted to encourage you.'

TWENTY EIGHT

I am now a consultant

The Ministry of Tourism in Rome had a problem. It seemed that hundreds of cats prowled the city's famous sites, scavenging food in trash cans and yowling at all hours. Tourism was declining and the number of complaints led the Ministry to conclude that the cats were the cause of the problem.

First, they decided to destroy all the cats, but someone suggested that they could save money if they destroyed only the cats of one sex. Without mates, the cat population would gradually decrease. Then someone suggested that they could save even more money if they did a study of the cat population and discovered which sex had fewer members. The study was completed and it was discovered that there were several hundred female cats and only one male cat who protected his territory with zeal. They decided to capture and destroy the male cat and thus solve their problem.

A newspaper picked up the story and reported it. Overnight the male cat, now named Rudolph, after Rudolph Valentino, became a local hero. Protestors marched in front of the Ministry of Tourism demanding that Rudolph be allowed to live. Faced with this opposition, the Ministry decided that instead of killing Rudolph, they would have him neutered. One night the fateful deed was done.

Soon the female cats discovered what had happened.

They began to call mournfully for their champion. Their yowling rang through the night. Neighbouring tomcats, learning that the city was now open to competition, began arriving from the surrounding areas. To their surprise, they found Rudolph strutting haughtily down the main thoroughfare, exacting tributes in return for allowing each tomcat entry to his domain.

"Why do you parade down the street with such pride when you can no longer perform?" he was asked.

"No longer am I an ordinary cat," he answered, "I am now a consultant."

TWENTY NINE

Is the Universe Friendly?

This famous question is attributed to Albert Einstein

"I think the most important question facing humanity is, 'Is the universe a friendly place?' This is the first and most basic question people must answer for themselves.

"For if we decide that the universe unfriendly, then we will use our technology, our scientific discoveries and our natural resources to achieve safety and power by creating bigger walls to keep out the unfriendliness and bigger weapons to destroy all that which is unfriendly and I believe that we are getting to a place where technology is powerful enough that we may either completely isolate or destroy ourselves as well in this process.

"If we decide that the universe is neither friendly nor unfriendly and that God is essentially 'playing dice with the universe', then we are simply victims to the random toss of the dice and our lives have no real purpose or meaning.

"But if we decide that the universe is a friendly place, then we will use our technology, our scientific discoveries and our natural resources to create tools and models for understanding that universe. Because power and safety will come through understanding its workings and its motives."

"God does not play dice with the universe."

THIRTY

Jack Sprat and his wife

Jack Sprat could eat no fat
His wife could eat no lean
And so betwixt the two of them
They licked the platter clean

Jack ate all the lean,
Joan ate all the fat.
The bone they picked it clean,
Then gave it to the cat

Two sisters and an orange

There is a classic fable of two sisters, quarrelling over a single orange.

Actually, the sisters were very keen not to quarrel, but to be fair to each other and to avoid any confrontation. So they agreed to cut the orange in half. Friendly, maybe, but it was actually a compromise. Then one sister used the juice and threw the rind away; the other sister used the rind and threw the juice away.

Too late, they realised that had they taken the trouble to ask what each other really needed, both sisters would have been far better off by giving all the juice to one sister and all the rind to the other sister.

THIRTY ONE

Knowing where to tap

A story told by Steve Andreas

There is an old story of a boilermaker who was hired to fix a huge steamship boiler system that was not working well.

The ship's owners had tried one expert after another, but none of them could figure out how to fix the engine. Then they brought in an old man who had been fixing ships since he was a youngster.

He carried a large bag of tools with him, and after listening to the engineer's description of the problems and asking a few questions, he went to the boiler room when he arrived, he immediately went to work.

He inspected the engine very carefully, top to bottom. He looked at the maze of twisting pipes, listened to the thump of the boiler and the hiss of escaping steam for a few minutes, and felt some pipes with his hands.

Then he hummed softly to himself, reached into his overalls and took out a small hammer, and tapped a bright red valve, once.

Immediately the entire system began working perfectly, and the boilermaker went home.

When the steamship owner received a bill for $1,000 he complained that the boilermaker had only been in the engine room for fifteen minutes, and requested an itemised bill.

This is what the boilermaker sent him:
For tapping with hammer: $0.50
For knowing where to tap: $999.50
Total: $1,000.00

THIRTY TWO

Learning to let go

There are many different rituals around the world for dealing with grief and how to mourn.

I have heard it told that in South America it used to be the practice that when a wife died, her husband would wrap her body in a sack and tie it to a sling so that he could carry the body on his back and yet continue with his normal work.

Since this was a hot country and there had been no effort to embalm the body, it would gradually begin to decompose.

And as it started to rot, so it would start to stink. As time went on the smell would get stronger and stronger, and more and more unpleasant.

Eventually it would become so bad that the widower would be desperate to get rid of his wife, and would finally cut the rope and let her go.

THIRTY THREE

Lexus customer service

A BMW owner walked into a Lexus dealership and announced that he was considering changing automobile brands. He had seen an ad about Lexus' legendary service. But first he had a service question for the Lexus salesperson.

"Earlier this week I took my BMW in for routine maintenance. In the process they removed the ashtray to clean it but forgot to put it back. When I discovered it was missing, I called the BMW service manager. He said they had indeed found the wayward ashtray shortly after I left and would be happy to hold it up from in the office for me to pick up at my convenience. Now, how would you have handled this situation?"

The Lexus sales person replied, "Well, sir, it would not have happened since we have a 54-item checklist that includes replacing the ashtray after cleaning. But, if it were to have happened, we would not have waited for you to call us."

The BMW owner smiled and left the showroom.

That afternoon after work, the Lexus salesperson drove to the BMW dealership, picked up the customer's ashtray, and surprised him with it at the front door of his home!

THIRTY FOUR

Life is what you make it

There's a story about a woman who did not keep a tidy house. One day someone gave her a beautiful rose which she brought home and put in a vase in her lobby. The rose, though, showed up the vase which was tarnished and dusty, so she polished the vase and set the rose and vase on the table.

But now something was wrong with the table. It looked terrible. It had to be cleaned as well. At last the woman stood back and admired the sparkling table, the polished vase, and the beautiful rose.

But to her dismay, the whole lobby and house now seemed dull and murky. Before she knew it, she found herself scrubbing the walls, washing the curtains, and opening the windows to let light and air into every dark corner.

THIRTY FIVE

Long spoons

After a certain man died, he was given a tour of both heaven and hell, so he could select his final destination. First he was taken to see Hell and the sight was horrifying. He saw a lot of people sitting at a long banquet table loaded with all kinds of delicious food. However, he noticed that all the people seated were unhappy, and looked frustrated.

Row after row of tables were laden with platters of sumptuous food, yet the people seated around the tables were pale and emaciated, moaning in hunger. As he came closer, he understood their predicament.

Every person held a full spoon, but both arms were splinted with wooden slats so he could not bend either elbow to bring the food to his mouth. It broke his heart to hear the tortured groans of these poor people as they held their food so near but could not consume it.

Next he was taken on a tour of Heaven. He was surprised to see the same setting he had witnessed in Hell – row after row of long tables laden with food. But in contrast to Hell, the people here in Heaven were sitting contentedly talking with each other, obviously sated from their sumptuous meal.

As he came closer, he was amazed to discover that here, too, each person had his arms splinted on wooden slats that prevented him from bending his elbows. How, then, did they manage to eat?

As he watched, a man picked up his spoon and dug it into the dish before him. Then he stretched across the table and fed the person across from him! The recipient of this kindness thanked him and returned the favour by leaning across the table to feed his benefactor.

THIRTY SIX

Mahatma Gandhi and sugar

There is a story told about Mahatma Gandhi

A lady brought her son and said he ate too much sugar. She wanted Gandhi to tell him to stop.   Gandhi said to bring the child back the next week.

The next week she brought the child and Gandhi said "Stop eating sugar child". And the child did.

A month later the lady came back and said "My child has done what you asked, but why could you not have spoken to him the first time I came."

"Lady", said Gandhi, "a week earlier I was still eating sugar".

THIRTY SEVEN

Michelangelo's David

Michelangelo is often quoted by trainers looking for a metaphor.

"In every block of marble I see a statue as plain as though it stood before me, shaped and perfect in attitude and action. I have only to hew away the rough walls that imprison the lovely apparition to reveal it to the other eyes as mine see it."

You can read the story behind this in the Appendix.

THIRTY EIGHT

Monkeys learn, monkeys teach

Five monkeys were placed in a cage where there was a bunch of bananas at the top of a step ladder.

Monkeys like bananas and soon one of them decided to climb the ladder to get himself some food.

When he was half way up, the experimenters sprayed him with a spray of freezing cold water. They also sprayed the rest of the monkeys.

The monkey quickly retreated. A little later another one tried. Once again he and the other monkeys were sprayed with cold water. Once again he gave up and retreated.

This was repeated every time a monkey tried to reach the bananas.

Eventually, they all gave up and ignored the bunch of bananas at the top of the ladder.

On another day the experimenters withdrew one of the monkeys and let a new monkey into the cage. Not surprisingly, he spotted the bananas and set out for the ladder. Before he could get halfway up the ladder, the other monkeys dragged him back. Every time that he attempted to reach the bananas, they stopped him, until he gave up.

The next day the experimenters withdrew another of the original monkeys and let in a new one.

The same thing happened as previously. The monkeys stopped the new monkey from getting to the bananas.

The experimenters repeated this exercise until all the original monkeys had been replaced.

Each day, the same thing happened. The monkeys that had been in the cage the day before stopped the new monkey from getting at the bananas. This happened even when none of the monkeys that had been exposed to the cold water was still in the cage.

The practice had been learned and passed on, even though there was neither evidence nor memory to support it.

THIRTY NINE

Peter's Laws

The Creed of the Sociopathic Obsessive Compulsive

1. If anything can go wrong. Fix it! (To hell with Murphy!)
2. When given a choice - take both!
3. Multiple projects lead to multiple successes.
4. Start at the top then work your way up.
5. Do it by the book...but be the author!
6. When forced to compromise, ask for more..
7. If you can't beat them, join them, then beat them.
8. If it's worth doing, it's got to be done right now.
9. If you can't win, change the rules.
10. If you can't change the rules, then ignore them.
11. Perfection is not optional.
12. When faced without a challenge, make one.
13. "No" simply means begin again at one level higher.
14. Don't walk when you can run.

15. Bureaucracy is a challenge to be conquered with a righteous attitude, a tolerance to stupidity, and a bulldozer when necessary.

16. When in doubt: THINK!

17. Patience is a virtue, but persistence to the point of success is a blessing.

18. The squeaky wheel gets replaced.

19. The faster you move, the slower time passes, the longer you live.

FORTY

Pavlov's Dogs

Ivan Pavlov was a noted Russian physiologist who went on to win the 1904 Nobel Prize for his work studying digestive processes. During the 1890s he was looking at salivation in dogs in response to being fed, when he noticed that his dogs would begin to salivate whenever the lab technician entered the room, even when he was not bringing them food. At first this was something of a nuisance (not to mention messy!).

Pavlov concluded that, rather than simply salivating in the presence of food, the dogs would begin to salivate in the presence of the lab technician who normally fed them.

From this observation he predicted that, if a particular stimulus in the dog's surroundings was present when the dog was given food, then this stimulus would become associated with food and cause salivation on its own.

He decided to test this out.

In his initial experiment, Pavlov used a bell to call the dogs to their food and, after a few repetitions, the dogs started to salivate in response to the bell. He called the bell the conditioned stimulus because its effect depended on its association with food. He called the food the unconditioned stimulus   because its effect did not depend on previous experience.

The timing between the presentation of the conditioned stimulus and the unconditioned stimulus is integral to facilitating the conditioned response. Pavlov found that the shorter the interval between the bell's ring and the appearance of the food, the more quickly the dog learned the conditioned response and the stronger it was.

FORTY ONE

Probability theory

There is a story about an old lady caught carrying a bomb onto an airplane. When accosted, she replied "I know that it is unlikely that there will be a terrorist bomb on this plane, but I have been told that probability theory says that the odds are very much greater against there being two bombs on the plane. I wanted to travel in greater safety."

FORTY TWO

Putting things into perspective

From *The Psychology of Influence and Persuasion*, Robert B Cialdini

Dear Mother and Dad

Since I left college I have been remiss in writing and I am sorry for my thoughtlessness in not having written before. I will bring you up to date now, but before you read on, please sit down. You are not to read any further unless you are sitting down, okay?

Well, then, I am getting along pretty well now. The skull fracture and the concussion I got when I jumped out the window of my dormitory when it caught fire shortly after my arrival here is pretty well healed now. I only spent two weeks in the hospital and now I can see almost normally and only get those sick headaches once a day. Fortunately, the fire in the dormitory, and my jump, was witnessed by an attendant at the gas station near the dorm, and he was the one who called the Fire Department and the ambulance. He also visited me in the hospital and since I had nowhere to live because of the burnt out dormitory, he was kind enough to invite me to share his apartment with him. It's really a base-ment room, but it's kind of cute. He is a very fine boy and we have fallen deeply in love and are planning to get married. We haven't got the exact date yet, but it will be before my pregnancy begins to show.

Yes, Mother and Dad, I am pregnant. I know how much you are looking forward to being grandparents and I know you will welcome the baby and give it the same love and devotion and tender care you gave me when I was a child. The reason for the delay in our marriage is that my boyfriend has a minor infection which prevents us from passing our pre-marital blood tests and I carelessly caught it from him.

Now that I have brought you up to date, I want to tell you that there was no dormitory fire, I did not have a concussion or skull fracture, I was not in hospital, I am not pregnant, I am not engaged, I am not infected, and there is no boyfriend. However, I am getting a "D" in American History, and an "F" in Chemistry and I want you to see those marks in their proper perspective.

Your loving daughter,
Sharon

FORTY THREE

Rattle snakes or gophers?

Here is a story from Michael Crichton

In the early seventies, flush with success from spinning his novel The Andromeda Strain into a critically and commercially acclaimed film, he bought a home in the hills of Los Angeles. A friend asked him if he was afraid of the snakes. "What snakes?" the author asked. The rattlesnakes, of course, which his friend told him, come out in force during the dry season.

Crichton returned to his magnificent new home in a complete funk and didn't have any fun at all. He just looked for snakes.

"I worried that snakes were sneaking into my bedroom, so I locked all the doors every night to keep the snakes out. I thought snakes might come to the swimming pool to drink the water, so I avoided the swimming pool, particularly in the heat of the day, because the snakes were probably sunning on my deck. I never walked around my property, because I was sure there were snakes in the bushes. I walked only on the little path on the side of the house, and I peered around every corner before I turned it.

"But, increasingly, I didn't like to go outside at all. I became a prisoner in my own house. I had altered my entire behaviour and my emotional state purely on the basis of something I had been told. I still hadn't seen any snakes. But I was now afraid."

One day he saw his gardener tramping fearlessly around the property. The author asked if there were any rattlers in the area. Sure, his gardener replied, especially in the dry season.

Wasn't he worried? The gardener shrugged and said he'd only seen a rattler once in over six years. He simply went and got a shovel and killed it. Only one snake in six years? Crichton's mood brightened. In rational terms, there was really nothing to be worried about. He sat by the pool for the rest of the day.

As the gardener was leaving, he told the author he could be sure there were no snakes on the property, because Crichton had so many gophers.

Gophers! The very critters that the recent homeowner had spent weeks setting traps for, trying to poison, and taking potshots at with his air rifle. All to no effect whatever. "Each morning fresh gopher burrows crisscrossed my lawn. It was extremely frustrating. My house looked like National Gopher Park."

Crichton began to rethink how to deal with the tunnelling terrors, and eventually the gophers' mortal enemies came to mind. "Was there anything I could do to attract rattlesnakes to my house? Put out some favourite rattlesnake food, or some dishes of water?"

FORTY FOUR

Rocks and the meaning of life

A philosophy professor stood before his class and had some items in front of him. When the class began, wordlessly he picked up a large empty mayonnaise jar and proceeded to fill it with rocks, rocks about 2" in diameter. He then asked the students if the jar was full? They agreed that it was.

So the professor then picked up a box of pebbles and poured them into the jar. He shook the jar lightly. The pebbles, of course, rolled into the open areas between the rocks. He then asked the students again if the jar was full. They agreed it was. The students laughed.

The professor picked up a box of sand and poured it into the jar. Of course, the sand filled up everything else.

"Now," said the professor, "I want you to recognise that this is your life. The rocks are the important things - your family, your partner, your health, your children - things that if everything else was lost and only they remained, your life would still be full. The pebbles are the other things that matter like your job, your house, your car. The sand is everything else, the small stuff. If you put the sand into the jar first, there is no room for the pebbles or the rocks. The same goes for your life. If you spend all your time and energy on the small stuff, you will never have room for the things that are important to you. Pay attention to the things that are critical to your happiness. Play with your children. Take time to get medical checkups. Take your partner out dancing. There will always be time to go to work, clean the house, give a dinner party and fix the disposal. Take care of the rocks first - the things that really matter. Set your priorities. The rest is just sand."

But then...

A student then took the jar which the other students and the professor agreed was full, and proceeded to pour in a glass of beer. Of course the beer filled the remaining spaces within the jar making the jar truly full.

The moral of this tale is:- no matter how full your life is, there is always room for BEER!

FORTY FIVE

Self appraisal

A little boy went to a telephone booth which was at the cash counter of a store and dialled a number. The store-owner observed and listened to the conversation:

Boy: "Lady, Can you give me the job of cutting your lawn?"

Woman: (at the other end of the phone line). "I already have someone to cut my lawn."

Boy: "Lady, I will cut your lawn for half the price than the person who cuts your lawn now."

Woman: "I'm very satisfied with the person who is presently cutting my lawn."

Boy: (with more perseverance) "Lady, I'll even sweep the floor and the stairs of your house for free."

Woman: "No, thank you."

With a smile on his face, the little boy replaced the receiver.

The store-owner, who was listening to all this, walked over to the boy.

Store Owner: "Son... I like your attitude; I like that positive spirit and would like to offer you a job."

Boy: "No thanks."

Store Owner: "But you were really pleading for one."

Boy: "No Sir, I was just checking my performance at the job I already have. I am the one who is working for that lady I was talking to."

This is called "Self Appraisal."

FORTY SIX

Shake it off and step up

Once upon a time there was a farmer who had an old mule. The mule fell into a deep dry well and began to cry loudly. Hearing his mule cry, the farmer came over and assessed the situation. The well was deep and the mule was heavy. He knew it would be difficult, if not impossible, to lift the animal out.

Because the mule was old and the well was dry, the farmer decided to bury the animal in the well. In this way he could solve two problems: put the old mule out of his misery and have his well filled.

He called on his neighbours to help him and they agreed to help. To work they went. Shovel full of dirt after shovel full of dirt began to fall on the mule's back. He became hysterical.

Then all of a sudden an idea came to the mule. Each time they would throw a shovelful of dirt on his back he could shake it off and step up. Shovelful after shovelful, the mule would shake it off and step up.

Now exhausted and dirty, but quite alive, the mule stepped over the top of the well and walked through the crowd.

FORTY SEVEN

Sharpen your axe

Once upon a time there two men who lived in the same forest decided to have a contest chopping wood.

The first man was in good physical shape and very muscular. The second man was in good shape but smaller in statute and wiry.

They would chop wood all day and at the end of the day compare to see who had chopped the most wood.

The first man laughed to himself that there was no way this wiry little man would beat him and so they began the contest.

Every 45 minutes the second smaller man would take a break and seems to just wonder off somewhere. The first man laughed again to himself and said "Yep there's no way this wiry little man is going to beat me."

This happens several times during the day.

At the end of the day the two men compare their piles of chopped wood and unbelievably enough the wiry little man has chopped twice as much wood as the more physically fit man.

He says "I don't understand. First I'm twice your size and twice your strength! On top of that every 45 minutes you rolled off and took a break or a nap or something. You must have cheated!"

The smaller man says "I don't cheat. It was easy to beat you because every 45 minutes when you thought I was taking a break, I was out back sharpening my axe."

FORTY EIGHT

Socrates and the story of the donkey

Socrates, the Ancient Greece philosopher, used to give public discourses about serious subjects like life and the after life while standing on a big stone in the corner of the market. People in the market and the passers by would come and listen for a few minutes and then leave when they realised he was talking about philosophy.

When Socrates, found that people were not giving much attention to his philosophy, he decided that he was going to tell a very interesting story. Then he started to tell his story. People who heard his announcement came near, very eager to hear his story.

It started like this. "A merchant who had a lot of merchandise to sell decided to go to another city so that he could get some extra profit from the business. He packed his goods and took them on his shoulder and left for another city before day break. He had to climb a big mountain to reach the other city. There was no other way but to climb the mountain with his merchandise.

"While he was walking he found another man with a donkey, also heading to the same city. They were walking together and talking to each other, and they became friends. Then the merchant asked the other man to rent his donkey to hold his merchandise till they reached the city. The man agreed for a certain amount of money."

At this point Socrates found that a large audience

had gathered around him to listen the story and a lot of people had forgotten their duty and were listening to his story instead. People who used to come and listen and leave within a few minutes also forgot their business and stayed back to listen to the story. Then he continued his story like this:

"They had to climb a steep mountain to reach their destination. The merchant placed his merchandise on the donkey and they started out in the morning. It was easy to walk in the morning. As the day progressed, it became very tough for them to climb the mountain. They were sweating and becoming very tired. But when the sun rose to above their heads they decided to take a rest."

Socrates found a large number of people gathered around him and very eagerly listening his story. He continued:

"It was 12 noon and they were tired. They decided to take a break. But there were no trees or shade under which they could sit and take rest, there was only the shade of the donkey that carrying the merchandise. Under the shade of that donkey there was space for only one man.

"The owner of the donkey told the other man that the shade of the donkey solely belonged to him as he was the owner of the donkey. But the merchant wanted to sit and take rest so he disagreed, saying that, since he had hired the donkey, the shade of the donkey solely belonged to him.

"The owner of the donkey replied that he had only let out the donkey, not the shade. But the merchant said that as long as he was hiring the donkey, the shade belonged to him. The men fell into a fierce argument for the shade of the donkey. Both argued that it belonged to them legally."

By this time there was a large crowd of people gathered around Socrates. So He climbed down from the stone where he was standing and walked away. People followed him demanding he complete the story. He paid no attention to them and continued his walking. People were following him and asking him to complete the story all the more.

They pressed him hard for the end of the story, so he stopped walking and turned to them and said. "I was talking to you people about great and serious things like life and the after life. But you were not paying any attention. But when I started to telling an imaginative story about a Donkey and its shade you are very eager to listen and want to know the end of the story. You are paying more attention to silly things and ignoring the important things in life. It is better for you to look for important things of life, do not run after silly things like stories. Do some important things every day and pursue it."

FORTY NINE

Something we can learn from geese

Adapted from the work of Dr. Angeles Arrien

Fact No. 1

As each bird flaps its wings it creates an uplift for the bird following. By flying in a "V" formation, the whole flock has 71% greater flying range than if the bird flew alone. Many of us recognise that there is a lot I can do by myself, there is a lot I can do with a colleague or partner, but the power of what I can get done with a network group is quantum.

The lesson from this fact - people who share a common direction and sense of community can get where they are going quicker and easier because they are travelling on the thrust of one another.

Fact No. 2

Whenever a goose falls out of formation, it suddenly feels the drag and resistance of trying to fly alone and quickly gets back into formation to take advantage of the lifting power of the bird immediately in front.

Lesson from this fact - if we have as much sense as a goose, we will stay in formation with those who are headed where we want to go and be willing to accept their help, as well as give ours to others who are looking for support.

Fact No. 3

When the lead goose gets tired, it rotates back into the formation and another goose flies at the point position - an invaluable lesson for us to apply to all our group work. It pays to take turns doing the hard tasks and sharing the leadership. With people, as with geese, we are inter-dependent on each other's skills and capabilities and unique arrangements of power and resources; no one person is right to lead in all circumstances and at all times.

Leaders need to learn to let go at times, and others must feel comfortable in stepping forward - no false modesty - no greed for power and position for its own sake.

Fact No. 4

When a goose becomes ill or wounded or shot down, two geese move out of formation and follow it down to help protect it. They stay with it until it is able to fly again or dies, then they launch out together with another forma-tion or they catch up with their flock.

Lesson - if we have as much sense as geese, we, too, will stand by each other in difficult times as well as when we are strong.

Fact No.5

The geese in formation honk from behind to encourage those up front to keep up their speed.

Lesson - we need to make sure our honking from behind is encouragement and not something else! In groups where there is great encouragement against great odds, the production is much greater by the power of encouragement.

The word "courage" means to stand by one's heart, to stand by one's core, to encourage someone else's core, to encourage someone else's heart - that's the quality of honking.

FIFTY

Speak to us of Children

From *The Prophet*, Kahlil Gibran

And a woman who held a babe against her bosom said, speak to us of children.

And he said:

> Your children are not your children.
>
> They are the sons and daughters of life's longing for itself.
>
> They come through you but not from you,
>
> And though they are with you they belong not to you.
>
> You may give them your love but not your thoughts,
>
> For they have their own thoughts.
>
> You may house their bodies but not their souls,
>
> For their souls dwell in the house of tomorrow,
>
> Which you cannot visit, not even in your dreams.
>
> You may strive to be like them, but not seek to make them like you.

For life goes not backward nor tarries with yesterday.

You are the bows from which your children as living arrows are sent forth.

The archer sees the mark upon the path of the infinite, and He bends you with His might that His arrows may go swift and far.

Let your bending in the Archer's hand be for gladness;

For even as He loves the arrow that flies, so He loves also the bow that is stable.

FIFTY ONE

Speak to us of Work

From *The Prophet*, Kahlil Gibran

Then a ploughman said, Speak to us of Work.

And he answered, saying:

Work is love made visible.

And if you cannot work with love but only with distaste, it is better that you should leave your work and sit at the gate of the temple and take alms of those who work with joy.

For if you bake bread with indifference, you bake a bitter bread that feeds but half a man's hunger.

And if you grudge the crushing of the grapes, your grudge distils a poison in the wine.

And if you sing though as angels, and love not the singing, you muffle man's ears to the voices of the day and the voices of the night.

FIFTY TWO

Speak to us of teaching

From *The Prophet*, Kahlil Gibran

Then said a teacher, Speak to us of Teaching.

And he said:

No man can reveal to you aught but that which already lies half asleep in the dawning of your knowledge.

The teacher who walks in the shadow of the temple, among his followers, gives not of his wisdom but rather of his faith and his lovingness.

If he is indeed wise he does not bid you enter the house of his wisdom, but rather leads you to the threshold of your mind.

The astronomer may speak to you of his understanding of space, but he cannot give you his understanding.

The musician may sing to you of the rhythm which is in all space, but he cannot give you the ear which arrests the rhythm, nor the voice that echoes it.

And he who is versed in the science of numbers can tell of the weight and measure, but he cannot conduct you thither.

For the vision of one mann lends not its wings to another man.

And even as each one of you stands alone in God's knowledge, so must each one of you be alone in his knowledge of God and in his understanding of the earth.

FIFTY THREE

Stone soup

There was once a village struck by famine and the people there were starving.

Children ran around on spindly legs, and as for animals, their ribs were sticking out so pathetically it was hard not to cry.

A kindly, old stranger was walking through the land when he came upon a village. As he entered, the villagers moved towards their homes locking doors and windows.

The stranger smiled and asked, "Why are you all so frightened? I am a simple traveller, looking for a soft place to stay for the night and a warm place for a meal."

The villagers grew wary when they heard this because who could feed one more mouth when they did not have enough for their own stomachs?

"Please go away. We do not have food for you. There's not a bite to eat in the whole province," he was told. "We are weak and our children are starving. Better keep moving on."

"Oh, I have everything I need," he said. "In fact, I was thinking of making some stone soup to share with all of you."

The villagers watched suspiciously as he built a fire and filled a cauldron with water. With great ceremony, he pulled a stone from a bag, dropping the stone into the pot of water. He sniffed the brew extravagantly and exclaimed how delicious the stone soup is.

"Ahh," the stranger said to himself rather loudly, "I do like a tasty stone soup. Of course, stone soup with cabbage - that's hard to beat."

Soon a villager approached hesitantly, holding a small cabbage he'd retrieved from its hiding place, and added it to the pot.

"Wonderful!" cried the stranger. "You know, I once had stone soup with cabbage and a bit of salt beef as well, and it was fit for a king."

The village butcher managed to find some salt beef. Then a villager remembered that he had some onions in the corner of his kitchen. A mother of three offered a few carrots she had hidden away against a crisis. Someone else poured in a handful of lentils.

Slowly, slowly, the soup grew thick, delicious and nourishing until there was a delicious meal for everyone in the village to share.

The village elders offered the stranger a great deal of money for the magic stone, but he refused to sell it and travelled on the next day.

Story of the man in the flood

A policeman called on a man in his home to warn him that the river level was rising and that his house would be flooded. He should gather a few things and leave immediately.

"No need," he replied. "I trust in God. He will save me."

The flood did come and the man had to move upstairs into a bedroom. A boat came along and approached the man at his window. "Please come with us, the water level is still rising."

"No need," he replied. "I trust in God. He will save me."

The water level rose further and he had to climb onto the roof. Eventually he was clinging to the chimney with water lapping at his feet.

A helicopter flew overhead and lowered a rescuer. "Please grab onto me and we'll winch you to safety."

"No need," he replied. "I trust in God. He will save me."

The water level continued to rise and the man drowned.

Having been a good man during his lifetime, he went to Heaven and was welcomed by St Peter at the Pearly Gates. "Welcome to Heaven" St Peter said. The man replied "Welcome indeed! I should not be here; I trusted in God but he did not save me."

"What do you mean?", St Peter said. "We sent a policeman to warn you, but you ignored him. We sent a boat to save you and you refused it. We sent a helicopter to rescue you and you refused that, too."

"What else could we have done for someone so stubborn? Welcome to Heaven."

FIFTY FIVE

Story of the runaway horse

This is a story told by Milton Erickson, one of the founders of psychotherapy

"I was returning from high school one day and a run-away horse with a bridle sped past a group of us into a farmer's yard... looking for a drink of water.

"The horse was perspiring heavily. And the farmer didn't recognise it, so we cornered it. I hopped on the horse's back... since it had a bridle on, I took hold of the rein and said, "Giddy-up..." and headed for the highway.

"I knew the horse would turn in the right direction... I didn't know what the right direction was.

"And the horse trotted and galloped along. Now and then he would forget he was on the highway and start into a field. So I would pull on him a bit and call his attention to the fact that the highway was where he was supposed to be.

"Finally, about four miles from where I had boarded him he turned into a farmyard and the farmer said, "So that's how that creature came back. Where did you find him?"

"I said, "About four miles from here."

"How did you know he should come here?"

"I said, 'I didn't know... the horse knew. All I did was keep his attention on the road.'"

FIFTY SIX

Story of two firemen

Extract from *The Zahir*, Paulo Coelho

"Marie, let's suppose that two firemen go into a forest to put out a small fire. Afterwards, when they emerge and go over to a stream, the face of one is all smeared with black, while the other man's face is completely clean. My question is this: which of the two will wash his face?"

"That's a silly question. The one with the dirty face of course."

"No, the one with the dirty face will look at the other man and assume that he looks like him. And, vice versa, the man with the clean face will see his colleague covered in grime and say to himself: I must be dirty too.
I'd better have a wash."

"What are you trying to say?"

"I'm saying that, during the time I spent in hospital, I came to realise that I was always looking for myself in the women I loved. I looked at their lovely, clean faces and saw myself reflected in them. They, on the other hand, looked at me and saw the dirt on my face and, however intelligent or self-confident they were, they ended up seeing themselves reflected in me and thinking that they were worse than they were. Please, don't let that happen to you."

Story of two travellers

One day a traveller was walking along a road on his journey from one village to another. As he walked, he noticed a monk tilling the ground in the fields beside the road. The monk greeted him and the traveller nodded to the monk.

The traveller then turned to the monk and said, "Excuse me, do you mind if I ask you a question?"

"Not at all," replied the monk.

"I have been staying in a village in the mountains and on my way to the village down there in the valley. Do you know what it is like there?"

"Tell me," said the monk. "What was your experience of the village in the mountains?"

"Dreadful," replied the traveller. "To be honest, I am glad to be away from there.

I found the people most unwelcoming. When I first arrived I was greeted coldly.

I was never made to feel a part of the village no matter how hard I tried.

The villagers keep very much to themselves; they don't take kindly to strangers.

What can I expect in the village in the valley?"

"I'm sorry to tell you," said the monk, "but I think your experience will be much the same there."

The traveller hung his head despondently and walked on.

A few weeks later, another traveller came along the same road and he also spoke to the monk.

"Good day," said the traveller.

"Good day," said the monk.

"How are you?" asked the traveller.

"I'm well," replied the monk. "Where are you going?"

"I'm going to the village in the valley," replied the traveller. "Do you know what it is like?"

"I do," replied the monk. "But first, tell me, where have you come from?"

"I've been staying in a village in the mountains."

"And how was that?"

"It was a wonderful experience. I would have stayed if I could but am committed to travelling on.

"I felt as though I were a member of the family in the village.

"The elders gave me much advice, the children laughed and joked with me, and the people generally were very kind and generous.

"I am sad to have left there. It will always hold special memories for me."

"And what of the village in the valley?" he asked again.

"I think you will find it much the same," replied the monk.

FIFTY EIGHT

Strive for balance in life

A quotation from Buckminster Fuller

"Imagine life as a game in which you are juggling some five balls in the air.

"You name them – work, family, health, friends and spirit and you're keeping all of these in the air. You will soon understand that work is a rubber ball. If you drop it, it will bounce back.

"But the other four balls – family, health, friends and spirit are made of glass. If you drop one of these, they will be irrevocably scuffed, marked, nicked, damaged or even shattered.

"They will never be the same. You must understand that and strive for balance in your life."

FIFTY NINE

Stuck in a hole

A man was walking along a sidewalk when he fell into an unprotected hole. He could not get out.

A doctor came along and he cried out for help. The doctor wrote him a prescription, threw it into the hole and continued walking.

Then a priest came along and he cried out again. This time, the priest wrote down a prayer, threw it into the hole and continued walking.

Finally, a friend came along. His response was to jump down into the hole to comfort the man.

The man said "What was the point of that? Now we are both stuck down the hole."

"Ah" replied his friend 'but I have been here before, and I know how to get out."

SIXTY

Tethered elephants

A tourist was doing a hike through the jungle, when he saw some large elephants tethered to a small stake.

He asked their trainer, "How can you keep such a large elephant tied to such a small stake?"

The trainer replied, "When the elephants are small, they try to pull out the stake and they fail. When they grow large, they never try to pull out the stake again."

SIXTY ONE

The blue tit and the milk bottle

From *The Living Company*, Arie de Geus

The United Kingdom has a long standing system of delivering milk in bottles to the door. At the beginning of the 20th century these milk bottles had no top. Birds had easy access to the cream which settled in the top of the bottle. Two different species of British garden birds, the blue tits and red robins, learned to siphon up cream from the bottles and tap this new, rich food source.

This innovation, in itself, was already quite an achievement. But it also had an evolutionary effect. The cream was much richer than the usual food sources of these birds, and the two species underwent some adaptation of their digestive systems to cope with the unusual nutrients. This internal adaptation almost certainly took place through Darwinian selection.

Then, between the two world wars, the UK dairy distributors closed access to the food source by placing aluminium seals on their bottles.

By the early 1950's the entire blue tit population of the UK, about a million birds, had learned how to pierce the aluminium seals. Regaining access to this rich food source provided an important victory for the blue tit family as a whole; it gave them an advantage in the battle for survival. Conversely, the robins, as a family, never regained access to the cream. Occasionally, an individual robin learns how to pierce the seals of the milk bottle. But the knowledge never passes to the rest of the species.

In short, the blue tits went through an extraordinarily successful institutional learning process. The robins failed, even though individual robins had been as innovative as individual blue tits. Moreover, the difference could not be attributed to their ability to communicate. As songbirds, both the blue tits and the robins had the same wide range of means of communication: colour, behaviour, movements, and song. The explanation could be found only in the social propagation process: the way blue tits spread their skill from one individual to members of the species as a whole.

In spring, the blue tits live in couples until they have reared their young. By early summer, when the young blue tits are flying and feeding on their own, we see birds moving from garden to garden in flocks of eight to ten individuals. These flocks seem to remain intact, moving together around the countryside, and the period of mobility lasts for two to three months.

Robins, by contrast, are territorial birds. A male robin will not allow another male to enter its territory. When threatened, the robin sends a warning, as if to say "Keep the hell out of here." In general, red robins tend to communicate with each other in an antagonistic manner, with fixed boundaries that they do not cross.

Birds that flock, seem to learn faster. They increase their chances to survive and evolve more quickly.

SIXTY TWO

The boy who cried wolf

This is an Aesop's Fable

There once was a shepherd boy who was bored as he sat on the hillside watching the village sheep. To amuse himself he took a great breath and sang out, "Wolf! Wolf! The Wolf is chasing the sheep!"

The villagers came running up the hill to help the boy drive the wolf away. But when they arrived at the top of the hill, they found no wolf. The boy laughed at the sight of their angry faces.

"Don't cry 'wolf', shepherd boy," said the villagers, "when there's no wolf!" They went grumbling back down the hill.

Later, the boy sang out again, "Wolf! Wolf! The wolf is chasing the sheep!" To his naughty delight, he watched the villagers run up the hill to help him drive the wolf away.

When the villagers saw no wolf they sternly said, "Save your frightened song for when there is really something wrong! Don't cry 'wolf' when there is NO wolf!"

But the boy just grinned and watched them go grumbling down the hill once more.

Later, he saw a REAL wolf prowling about his flock. Alarmed, he leaped to his feet and sang out as loudly as he could, "Wolf! Wolf!"

But the villagers thought he was trying to fool them

again, and so they didn't come.

At sunset, everyone wondered why the shepherd boy hadn't returned to the village with their sheep. They went up the hill to find the boy. They found him weeping.

"There really was a wolf here! The flock has scattered! I cried out, "Wolf!" Why didn't you come?"

An old man tried to comfort the boy as they walked back to the village.

"We'll help you look for the lost sheep in the morning," he said, putting his arm around the youth, "Nobody believes a liar... even when he is telling the truth!"

SIXTY THREE

The butterfly garden

This is a story told by Roger Hamilton. His story is to help understand the difference between people who are trying to make money and people who are building wealth.

He asks the question: "How is the best way to catch butterflies?"

Butterflies never stay in one place, but keep flying around. How do you catch them? One way to do this is to obtain a very large net and a long pole. Then you can run around attempting to catch them, one by one.

And once you have caught a few butterflies you have to struggle to hold onto them. Similarly, people who focus on making money use different strategies but then struggle to hold onto the money that they have earned.

An alternative approach is to focus on creating a beautiful garden. If you create something permanent around yourself, this attracts a large number of butterflies, birds, and bees. Even if some butterflies fly away, there will be more the next day. And also, there are other visitors who enrich the garden.

Likewise, even if wealth builders lose money, they gain more as they have a powerful network, a knowledge base, a resource base and a track record.

SIXTY FOUR

The butterfly's struggle

A man found a cocoon for a butterfly. One day a small opening appeared, he sat and watched the butterfly for several hours as it struggled to force its body through the little hole. Then it seemed to stop making any progress. It appeared as if it had gotten as far as it could and could go no farther. So the man decided to help the butterfly.

He took a pair of scissors and snipped the remaining bit of the cocoon. The butterfly emerged easily. But something was strange. The butterfly had a swollen body and shrivelled wings. The man continued to watch the butterfly because he expected at any moment, the wings would enlarge and expand to be able to support the body, which would contract in time. Neither happened. In fact, the butterfly spent the rest of its life crawling around with a swollen body and deformed wings. It was never able to fly.

What the man in his kindness and haste did not understand, was that the restricting cocoon and the struggle required for the butterfly to get through the small opening of the cocoon are nature's way of forcing fluid from the body of the butterfly into its wings so that it would be ready for flight once it achieved its freedom from the cocoon.

Sometimes struggles are exactly what we need in our life.

The country of the blind

Original story by H G Wells

While climbing in the mountains Nunez slipped and fell down a snow-slope into a valley cut off from the rest of the world on all sides by steep precipices. Unbeknown to Nunez, he had discovered the fabled Country of the Blind. The valley had been a haven for settlers fleeing the tyranny of Spanish rulers until an earthquake reshaped the surrounding mountains and cut it off forever. The isolated community prospered over the years despite a disease that struck them early on, rendering all newborns blind. As the blindness slowly spread over the generations, their remaining senses sharpened, and by the time the last sighted villager had died, the community had fully adapted to life without sight.

Nunez descended into the valley and found an unusual village with windowless houses and a network of paths, all bordered by kerbs. Upon discovering that everyone was blind, Nunez began reciting to himself the refrain, "In the Country of the Blind the One-Eyed Man is King". He realised that he could teach and rule them, but the villagers had no concept of sight and did not understand his attempts to explain this fifth sense to them. Frustrated, Nunez became angry but they calmed him and he reluctantly submitted to their way of life because returning to the outside world was impossible.

Nunez was assigned to work for a villager named Yacob, and became attracted to Yacob's youngest daughter, Medina-saroté. Nunez and Medina-saroté soon fell in love with one another, and having won her confidence, Nunez slowly started trying to explain sight to her. Medina-saroté, however, simply dismissed it as his imagination.

When Nunez asked for her hand in marriage he was turned down by the village elders on account of his "unstable" obsession with "sight". The village doctor suggested that Nunez's eyes be removed, claiming that they were diseased and were affecting his brain.

Nunez reluctantly consented to the operation because of his love for Medina-saroté. But at sunrise on the day of the operation, while all the villagers were asleep, Nunez, the failed King of the Blind, set off for the mountains, hoping to find a passage to the outside world and escape the valley.

After a while he noticed that there was about to be a rock slide. He ran back to the village to warn the villagers, but again they scoffed at his "imagined" sight.

Nunez took Medina-saroté and fled the valley during the slide.

SIXTY SIX

The cow in the ditch

When everything gets really complicated and you feel overwhelmed, think about it this way: You gotta do three things.

First, get the cow out of the ditch.

Second, find out how the cow got into the ditch.

Third, make sure you do whatever it takes so the cow doesn't go into the ditch again.

The Daffodil Principle

Several times a daughter had telephoned her mother to say, "Mother, you must come to see the daffodils before they are over."

She would have liked to go, but it was a two-hour drive to her daughter's.

"I will come next Tuesday", the mother promised a little reluctantly on her third call.

Next Tuesday dawned cold and rainy. Still, she had promised, and reluctantly she drove there. When she finally walked into her daughter's house she was welcomed by the joyful sounds of happy children. She delightedly hugged and greeted her grandchildren.

"Forget the daffodils! The road is invisible in these clouds and fog, and there is nothing in the world except you and these children that I want to see badly enough to drive another inch!"

The daughter smiled calmly and said, "We drive in this all the time, Mother."

"Well, you won't get me back on the road until it clears, and then I'm heading for home!" was the reply.

"But first we're going to see the daffodils. It's just a few blocks," the daughter said. "I'll drive. I'm used to it."

The mother replied sternly, "It's not worth it."

"It's all right, Mother," she promised. "You will never forgive yourself if you miss this experience."

After about twenty minutes, they turned onto a small

gravel road and saw a small church. On the far side of the church, there was a hand lettered sign with an arrow that read, "Daffodil Garden."

They got out of the car, each took a child's hand, and the daughter led them down the path. Then, as they turned a corner, the mother looked up and gasped. Before them lay the most glorious sight.

It looked as though someone had taken a great vat of gold and poured it over the mountain and its surrounding slopes. The flowers were planted in majestic, swirling patterns, great ribbons and swaths of deep orange, creamy white, lemon yellow, salmon pink, and saffron and butter yellow. Each different coloured variety was planted in large groups so that it swirled and flowed like its own river with its own unique hue. There were five acres of flowers.

"Who did this?" she asked her daughter. "Just one woman," was the reply. "She lives on the property. That's her home." The daughter pointed to a well-kept small A-frame house, modestly sitting in the midst of all that glory.

They walked up to the house.

On the patio, there was a poster. "Answers to the Questions I Know You Are Asking", was the headline. The first answer was a simple one. "50,000 bulbs," it read. The second answer was, "One at a time, by one woman. Two hands, two feet, and one brain." The third answer was, "Began in 1958."

Almost fifty years before, this unknown woman had begun, one bulb at a time, to bring her vision of beauty and joy to an obscure mountaintop. Planting one bulb at a time, year after year, this woman had forever changed the world in which she lived. One day at a time, she had created something of extraordinary magnificence, beauty, and inspiration.

SIXTY EIGHT

The frog in hot water

They say that if you put a frog into a pot of boiling water, it will leap out right away to escape the danger.

But, if you put a frog in a kettle that is filled with water that is cool and pleasant, and then you gradually heat the kettle until it starts boiling, the frog will not become aware of the threat until it is too late.

The frog's survival instincts are geared towards detecting sudden changes.

SIXTY NINE

The great corporate regatta

The Americans and the Japanese decided to engage in a competitive boat race.

Both teams practised hard and long to reach their peak performance.

On the big day they felt ready. The Japanese won by a mile. Afterward, the American team was discouraged by the loss. Morale sagged.

Corporate management decided that the reason for the crushing defeat had to be found,
so a consulting firm was hired to investigate the problem and recommended
corrective action.

The consultant's finding: The Japanese team had eight people rowing and one person steering; the American team had one person rowing and eight people steering.

After a year of study and millions spent analysing the problem, the consultant firm concluded that too many people were steering and not enough were rowing on the American team.

So as race day neared again the following year, the American team's management structure was completely reorganised. The new structure: four steering managers, three area steering managers and a new performance review system for the person rowing the boat to provide work incentive.

The next year, the Japanese won by two miles. Humiliated, the American corporation laid off the rower for poor performance and gave the managers a bonus for discovering the problem.

SEVENTY

The hungry perch experiment

There was an experiment in Norway with some fish in a tank.

A special tank was fabricated with a removable glass panel that divided it into two halves.

It was filled with water and a perch was placed in one half. In the other half were put some tasty minnows.

When the perch saw the minnows, it immediately swam towards them, only to get a 'bloody nose' when it hit the glass panel.

It withdrew in shock. But it was still hungry, and the minnows were enticingly active. So he had another go, and got another bloody nose. He swam around in his own part of the tank for a while, but eventually had yet another go. Same unfortunate result.

He continued to try, but with increasingly long intervals, until finally he gave up.

Then, the experimenters removed the glass panel. The perch continued to swim in its own half of the tank,and the minnows continued to swim in theirs, completely safe and unmolested.

SEVENTY ONE

The janitor at NASA

There is a story about a group of students from Harvard Business School who visited NASA at Houston in the 1960s to learn about the application of vision, mission and values in practice.

Two of the party were talking in the men's restroom, where a janitor was mopping the floor.

One said to the other: "We have heard all about NASA's vision, mission and values, let's test it out in practice. Let's ask this janitor what he is doing here."

They did this and were pleased to receive the reply: "I am helping to put a man on the moon."

SEVENTY TWO

The lighthouse and
the naval vessel

Unfortunately, it appears that this is another urban legend, but useful, nonetheless.

Through the pitch-black night, the captain of a US naval ship sees a light dead ahead on a collision course with his ship. He sends a signal: "Change your course 15 degrees north."

Canadians: "Please divert your course 15 degrees to the south to avoid a collision."

Americans: "Recommend you divert your course 15 degrees to the north."

Canadians: "Negative. You will have to divert your course 15 degrees to the south to avoid a collision."

Angry, the captain sends: "I'm a navy captain! Change your course, sir!"

"No Sir" comes the reply. "I recommend you change your course."

Now the captain is furious. "This is the captain of a US navy ship. I say again, divert YOUR course.

Canadians: "Calm down Sir, this is the Cape Race Lighthouse. It is Your call."

SEVENTY THREE

The marshmallow test

In a psychological experiment several young children were sat in front of a marshmallow and told that they could eat it now. However, if they could resist eating it until the researcher returned, they would then be given two marshmallows to eat. The researcher then left the room, though the behaviour of the children was caught on camera.

The kids could be seen squirming, wriggling, singing aloud and covering their eyes to distract themselves from the temptation; they might even allow themselves to sniff or slyly stroke the yummy dessert, but not pick it up: their cuteness was often irresistible.

However, in most cases they could not resist and at some stage while the researcher was out they succumbed to temptation and ate the marshmallow.

Follow up research indicated that the children who were able to restrain themselves long enough to earn the two marshmallows were generally those who ended up more successful later on in life: they grew up to achieve higher SAT scores (a 210 point difference), earn higher incomes, and have a lower chance of obesity, a lower risk of drug misuse and better health overall.

You can read a full report of the experiment and long term follow-up in the Appendix.

SEVENTY FOUR

The Mexican fisherman

An American investment banker was at the pier of a small coastal Mexican village when a small boat with just one fisherman docked. Inside the small boat were several large yellow fin tuna. The American complimented the Mexican on the quality of his fish and asked how long it took to catch them.

The Mexican replied, "only a little while".

The American then asked why didn't he stay out longer and catch more fish?

The Mexican said he had enough to support his family's immediate needs.

The American then asked, "but what do you do with the rest of your time?"

The Mexican fisherman said, "I sleep late, fish a little, play with my children, take siesta with my wife, Maria, stroll into the village each evening where I sip wine and play guitar with my amigos, I have a full and busy life."

The American scoffed, "I am a Harvard MBA and could help you. You should spend more time fishing and with the proceeds, buy a bigger boat. With the proceeds from the bigger boat you could buy several boats, eventually you would have a fleet of fishing boats. Instead of selling your catch to a middleman you would sell directly to the processor, eventually opening your own cannery. You would control the product, processing and distribution. You would need to leave this small coastal fishing village and move to Mexico City, then LA and eventually NYC where you will run your expanding enterprise."

The Mexican fisherman asked, "But, how long will this all take?"

To which the American replied, "15-20 years."

"But what then?"

The American laughed and said that's the best part. "When the time is right you would announce an IPO and sell your company stock to the public and become very rich, you would make millions."

"Millions. Then what?"

The American said, "Then you would retire. Move to a small coastal fishing village where you would sleep late, fish a little, play with your kids, take siesta with your wife, stroll to the village in the evenings where you could sip wine and play your guitar with your amigos."

SEVENTY FIVE

The miser

This story is from Aesop's Fables

A miser sold all that he had and bought a lump of gold, which he buried in a hole in the ground by the side of an old wall. Every day he would go and look at it.

One of his workmen observed his frequent visits to the spot and decided to watch his movements. He soon discovered the secret of the hidden treasure, and digging down, came to the lump of gold, and stole it.

On his next visit, the miser found the hole empty and began to tear his hair and to make loud lamentations.

A neighbour, seeing him overcome with grief and learning the cause, said, "Pray do not grieve so; but go and take a stone, and place it in the hole, and fancy that the gold is still lying there. It will do you quite the same service; for when the gold was there, you had it not, as you did not make the slightest use of it."

SEVENTY SIX

The NASA space pen

During the height of the space race in the 1960s, legend has it, NASA was faced with a major problem.

Their scientists realised that pens could not function in the vacuum of space. The astronauts needed a way to write things down.

They spent years and 1.5 million taxpayer dollars to develop a pen that could put ink to paper without gravity. It enjoyed minor success on the commercial market.

The Russians were faced with the same problem. They simply handed their cosmonauts pencils.

The real story and explanation can be found in the Appendix.

SEVENTY SEVEN

The parable of the porpoise

This story told by Gregory Bateson was reported by Robert Dilts

Anthropologist Gregory Bateson studied the communication patterns of dolphins and porpoises. He reports on his observation of training porpoises.

The trainer would wait until the porpoise did something unusual say, lifting its head out of the water in a certain way. The trainer would then blow a whistle and give the porpoise a fish. The trainer would then wait until the porpoise eventually repeated the behaviour, blow the whistle again and give it a fish. Soon the porpoise had learned what to do to get the fish and was lifting its head quite often, providing a successful demonstration of its ability to learn.

On the next day, the porpoise would repeat the trick. The trainer didn't want it to do the same old trick, but to learn a new one. So this time it did not get a fish. The porpoise would repeat it several times without reward until in frustration it would do something else, like flipping its tail.

The trainer immediately blew the whistle and threw it a fish. The surprised and somewhat confused porpoise cautiously flipped its tail again, and again got the whistle and a fish. Soon it was merrily flipping its tail, successfully demonstrating again its ability to learn.

At the third session the porpoise began dutifully flipping its tail as it had learned in the previous session. Once again, it was not rewarded. Once more the porpoise repeated the tricks it had learned until finally, out of exasperation, it did something different, such as spinning itself around. The trainer immediately sounded the whistle and gave the porpoise a fish. After some time it successfully learned to spin itself around.

The pattern continued for a fortnight. Every day the porpoise would repeat yesterday's trick without reward, become frustrated, and do something else. If the behaviour was a new one, the trainer blew her whistle and threw the porpoise a fish. By the end of the fourteenth day, the porpoise had developed and practised a repertoire of 14 tricks.

Finally, in between the fourteenth and fifteenth session, the porpoise would seem to become almost wild with excitement, as if it had suddenly discovered a goldmine. And when it was let into the exhibition tank for the fifteenth show it put on an elaborate performance including many completely original behaviours. One animal even exhibited eight completely new behaviours, including four of which which had never been observed in its species before.

The porpoise had leaned not only how to generate new behaviours, but the rules governing where, when and how to generate them.

Bateson mentioned one other powerful insight into the mechanisms of learning. Outside of the training environment during the first fortnight of training, Bateson would sometimes see the trainer throwing the porpoise an unearned fish. When he enquired why this was so, the trainer replied, "To keep the relationship with him. If I don't build a relationship with the porpoise, he's not going to bother to learn anything."

SEVENTY EIGHT

The parable of the talents

Matthew 25:14-30

This is a story told by Jesus about a man going on a long journey that would keep him away from home. Before he left, he called his servants together and entrusted his property to them.

To one he gave five talents of money, to another two talents, and to another one talent, each according to his ability. Then he went on his journey.

The man who had received the five talents went at once and put his money to work and gained five more. So also, the one with the two talents gained two more. But the man who had received the one talent went off, dug a hole in the ground and hid his master's money.

After a long time, the master of those servants returned and settled accounts with them. The man who had received the five talents brought the other five. "Master," he said, "you entrusted me with five talents. See, I have gained five more."

His master replied, "Well done, good and faithful servant! You have been faithful with a few things; I will put you in charge of many things. Come and share your master's happiness!"

The man with the two talents also came. "Master," he said, "you entrusted me with two talents; see, I have gained two more."

His master replied, "Well done, good and faithful servant! You have been faithful with a few things; I will put you in charge of many things. Come and share your master's happiness!"

Then the man who had received the one talent came. "Master," he said, "I knew that you are a hard man, harvesting where you have not sown and gathering where you have not scattered seed. So I was afraid and went out and hid your talent in the ground. See, here is what belongs to you."

His master replied, "You wicked, lazy servant! So you knew that I harvest where I have not sown and gather where I have not scattered seed? Well then, you should have put my money on deposit with the bankers, so that when I returned I would have received it back with interest.

"Take the talent from him and give it to the one who has the ten talents. For everyone who has will be given more, and he will have an abundance. Whoever does not have, even what he has will be taken from him. And throw that worthless servant outside, into the darkness, where there will be weeping and gnashing of teeth."

SEVENTY NINE

The power of a limiting belief

A young cowherd used to take his cows to the meadows every morning and bring them back to the cowshed at the end of the day.

One evening, as he was tying the cows up for the night, the boy found that one of them was missing her rope. He feared that she might run away, but it was too late to go and buy a new rope.

The boy didn't know what to do, so he went to a wise man who lived nearby and sought his advice.

The wise man told the boy to pretend to tie the cow, and make sure that the cow saw him doing it. He did as the wise man said and pretended to tie the cow.

The next morning the boy discovered that the cow had remained still throughout the night. He untied all the cows as usual, and they all went outside.

He was about to go to the meadows when he noticed that the cow with the missing rope was still in the cowshed. She was standing on the same spot where she had been all night. He tried to coax her to join the herd, but she wouldn't budge.

The boy was perplexed. He went back to the wise man who said, "The cow still thinks she is tied up. Go back and pretend to untie her."

The boy did as he was told, and the cow happily left the cowshed.

EIGHTY

The power of goal setting

I have found several versions of this story based on Harvard in 1953, or was it Yale, and another based on Harvard in 1979. The probability is that it is a management myth. However, don't let the truth get in the way of a good story!

I have combined versions and the story goes like this.

In 1953, Harvard decided to conduct a survey of all the students that were leaving that year. There were lots of questions in the survey asking about all manner of things like religious and political preferences and many other things too.

One of the questions was: "Have you set clear, written goals for your future and made plans to accomplish them?"

Only three percent of the graduates had written goals and plans; 13 percent had goals, but they were not in writing; and a whopping 84 percent had no specific goals at all.

Fast forward, twenty years: the university decided to run another survey. Originally, they were simply going to repeat the same study, but someone had the bright idea of using the money differently. They decided to contact all the students that had left twenty years earlier and see what they were up to.

It was a massive research project. Some of the students had died, but they found all of the remainder.

When they analysed the data, they discovered that the 13 percent of the class who had goals were earning, on average, twice as much as the 84 percent who had no goals at all.

And what about the three percent who had a habit of setting and writing goals as students, and then continued to write goals and review them regularly? They were earning, on average, ten times as much as the other 97 percent put together.

EIGHTY ONE

The quarrelling couple

This is a story told by Devdas Menon

Once upon a time there was a couple, husband and wife, who, like many other couples, would always quarrel and fight with each other.

So much so that one day the husband got so exasperated that he just walked out of the house. He couldn't take it any more and he just stormed out.

As he walked out he walked around and he found himself outside what looked like a temple, a Vishnu temple. He had never been there before. He walked in.

There was nobody inside; just the idol in front of him. He had never been very religious but lo and behold Lord Vishnu gave him a a personal direct instruction. He said "You may ask for three requests."

He said I can only ask for one request now, that is in my mind.

"What is it?"

He said "Help me get rid of my wife."

Vishnu smiled and said, "You really want that?"

"Yes," he replied.

He went back to his house and had a pleasant surprise. His wife had packed her bags and was waiting for him. She said "I am fed up with you. I am going." He said, "You really want to go?" She said, "Yes, I am going."

He was inwardly happy to see the end of her.

He wanted to celebrate so he called all his friends over. They asked him "What have you done? You should see our wives. Your wife is such a noble, gracious lady compared to them. She cooks good food and …"

Once they start talking about her he begins to realise that he has made a big mistake and asks his friends what to do.

They reply, "Forget it, we don't want a friend like you. We can't even have good food in your house." And they leave.

He gets frustrated and once again goes out walking and finds himself in front of the temple.

He goes inside. Once again there is nobody inside and Vishnu appears in front of him and asks him whether he is ready for his second request. He says "yes", but with a long face. He says "I want to get my wife back."

Vishnu says "Is that really what you want?" He says, "Yes."

He goes back home and again has a pleasant surprise. His wife has come back with all her luggage. She prostrates herself in front of him and asks for his forgiveness.

When they go in he confesses to her. He says, "Look there is something happening that I don't understand." He tells her the story.

Then he says, "Look, we have one request left. What should we ask for?" They are confused, so they go around their friends and relatives asking for advice. They got lots of opinions.

Some said "100,000 is not enough."

Others said "Ask for all the gold in the world." There were lots of ideas like this.

Others said, "You might die tomorrow, you should ask for health and wealth."

He was confused but clear about one thing, nobody knew what he should ask for.

He went boldly back to the temple. Once again Vishnu was there, smiling as usual. "Are you ready for your third request?" he asked.

He replied, "Yes, and no. Can you permit me to ask you one question before that?" Vishnu replied, "OK. If that is what you want."

He said, "I am totally confused and I know that I am being tested, and I have no faith in anybody, but I have faith in you. So, tell me 'What is it that I should ask of you that is in my best interest."

Vishnu said, "You might not like the answer."

He replied "I don't care. I have reached the pits in my life and I know that you will show me the right way."

Here is Vishnu's reply.

He said, "Ask that you be contented with whatever you have."

And so he asked, and so he received.

When he stepped out of the temple the world looked completely different. For the first time in his life he noticed shining green leaves on the trees. He saw the deer that had always been there. He saw the clouds and noticed the freshness in the air.

When he went home his wife didn't look like the old wife; she was beautiful, and there was a glow permeating from everything.

Something had happened, though nothing had happened.

The couple lived happily ever after.

EIGHTY TWO

The sower and the seed

This is a parable told by Jesus

A farmer went out to sow some seed. As he scattered the seed, some fell by the wayside, and birds came and ate it up.

Some of the seed fell on shallow and stony ground, where there was not much earth. Although it initially sprang up, when the sun was up, it was scorched; and because it had no root, it withered away.

More seed fell where there were thorns; the thorns grew up, and choked it, and it also yielded no fruit.

And some seed fell on fertile ground, where it was able to develop deep roots. This seed was able to germinate and grow, producing a crop thirty, sixty, or even a hundredfold, of what had been sown.

EIGHTY THREE

The story of the 100th Monkey

Although this story was first reported in a scientific paper, further investigation suggests that the conclusions are not justified. However, it has become popular in New Age literature.

The Japanese monkey Macaca Fuscata had been observed in the wild for a period of over thirty years. In 1952, on the island of Koshima, scientists were providing monkeys with sweet potatoes dropped in the sand. The monkeys liked the taste of the raw sweet potatoes but they found the dirt unpleasant.

An 18 month old female named Imo found she could solve the problem by washing the potatoes in a nearby stream. She taught this trick to her mother. Her playmates also learned this new way and they taught their mothers too. This cultural innovation was gradually picked up by various monkeys before the eyes of the scientists.

Between 1952 and 1958, all the young monkeys learned to wash the sandy sweet potatoes to make them more palatable. Only the adults who imitated their children learned this social improvement ... other adults kept eating the dirty sweet potatoes.

Then something startling took place. In the autumn of 1958 a certain number of Koshima monkeys were washing sweet potatoes - the exact number is not known. Let us suppose that when the sun rose one morning there were 99 monkeys on Koshima Island who had learned to wash their sweet potatoes. Let's further suppose that later that evening the hundredth monkey learned to wash potatoes ... THEN IT HAPPENED. By that evening almost everyone in the tribe was washing sweet potatoes before eating them. The added energy of this hundredth monkey somehow created an ideological breakthrough!

But notice. A most surprising thing observed by these scientists was that the habit of washing sweet potatoes then jumped over the sea - colonies of monkeys on other islands and the mainland troop of monkeys at Takasakiyama began washing their sweet potatoes.

Thus, when a certain number achieves an awareness, this new awareness may be communicated from mind to mind.

Although the exact number may vary, The Hundredth Monkey phenomenon means that when only a limited number of people know of a new way, it may remain the conscious property of just those people. But there is a point at which if only one more person tunes in to a new awareness, a field is strengthened so that this awareness is picked up by almost everyone!

Your awareness is needed. You may be the "hundredth monkey".

EIGHTY FOUR

The successful frog

A group of frogs were traveling through the woods, and two of them fell into a deep pit. All the other frogs gathered around the pit. When they saw how deep the pit was, they told the unfortunate frogs they would never get out. The two frogs ignored the comments and tried to jump up out of the pit.

The other frogs kept telling them to stop, that they were as good as dead. Finally, one of the frogs took heed to what the other frogs were saying and simply gave up. He fell down and died.

The other frog continued to jump as hard as he could. Once again, the crowd of frogs yelled at him to stop the pain and suffering and just die. He jumped even harder and finally made it out. When he got out, the other frogs asked him, "Why did you continue jumping. Didn't you hear us?"

The frog explained to them that he was deaf. He thought they were encouraging him the entire time.

EIGHTY FIVE

The sun and the moon

The sun and the wind were arguing about who was more powerful.

They decided to have a trial of strength and, looking down, they saw a man wearing a coat. They decided that whoever could get the coat off the man would have proved to be stronger.

The wind went first and blew and blew. But the more fiercely it blew, the more the man held his coat tightly around him.

Eventually, the wind invited the sun to have a try.

The sun simply shone on the man, who got hotter and hotter and took the coat off himself.

The therapy business

This is a story about a New York businessman who decided that he needed to consult a therapist.

He consulted the best sources to find a psychotherapist with an excellent reputation and very impressive fees. He made an appointment and turned up at the consulting rooms for his first session.

He was called into the room, which was very elegant and featured a flat couch on which he was invited to lie down.

"Please lie down on your back and make yourself comfortable. If anything comes into your mind that you would like to share, please feel free to do so," said the therapist. "If nothing comes into your mind, then that is OK, too."

He duly lay down as instructed, but nothing came into his mind so he lay in silence. After 45 minutes, the therapist told him that the session was completed and he could go now.

A week later he returned and the same procedure was followed. Once again, nothing came into his mind, so he said nothing. After 45 minutes the session ended and he left.

The next week he returned; same procedure.

And the next week, and the next week.

On the eight week he returned and lay down as he was accustomed. As usual, the therapist told him to make himself comfortable. "If there is anything you would like to raise with me, please feel free."

This time, when the end of the session arrived, he did have something to say. "Yes, doctor. I wonder, would you like a partner?"

EIGHTY SEVEN

The tortoise and the hare

Once upon a time there was a hare who, boasting how he could run faster than anyone else, was forever teasing tortoise for its slowness.

Then one day, the irate tortoise answered back: "Who do you think you are? There's no denying you're swift, but even you can be beaten!" The hare squealed with laughter.

"Beaten in a race? By whom? Not you, surely! I bet there's nobody in the world that can win against me, I'm so speedy. Now, why don't you try?"

Annoyed by such bragging, the tortoise accepted the challenge. A course was planned, and the next day at dawn they stood at the starting line. The hare yawned sleepily as the meek tortoise trudged slowly off. When the hare saw how painfully slow his rival was, he decided, half asleep on his feet, to have a quick nap. "Take your time!" he said. "I'll have forty winks and catch up with you in a minute."

The hare woke with a start from a fitful sleep and gazed round, looking for the tortoise. But the creature was only a short distance away, having barely covered a third of the course. Breathing a sigh of relief, the hare decided he might as well have breakfast too, and off he went to munch some cabbages he had noticed in a near-by field.

But the heavy meal and the hot sun made his eyelids

droop. With a careless glance at the tortoise, now halfway along the course, he decided to have another snooze before flashing past the winning post. And smiling at the thought of the look on the tortoise's face when it saw the hare speed by, he fell fast asleep and was soon snoring happily.

The sun started to sink below the horizon and the tortoise, who had been plodding towards the winning post since morning, was scarcely a yard from the finish.

At that very point, the hare woke with a jolt. He could see the tortoise a speck in the distance and away he dashed. He leapt and bounded at a great rate, his tongue lolling, and gasping for breath. Just a little more and he'd be first at the finish.

But the hare's last leap was just too late, for the tortoise had beaten him to the winning post.

Poor hare! Tired and in disgrace, he slumped down beside the tortoise who was silently smiling at him. "Slowly does it every time!" he said.

This story is from Aesop's Fables

EIGHTY EIGHT

The watermelon dragon

Many years ago in the hills of Tibet there was a village. Its inhabitants were starving. They lived in fear of a dragon that they had seen in their fields and they would not go to harvest their crops.

One day a traveller came to the village and asked for food. They explained that they had not enough for themselves because they were afraid of the dragon in their fields. The traveller was brave and offered to slay the dragon.

When he arrived in the fields he couldn't see a dragon, only a large watermelon.

So he returned to the village and said, "You have nothing to fear; there is no dragon, only a large watermelon."

The villagers were angry at his refusal to understand their fear and hacked the traveller to pieces.

Some days later another traveller came to the village.

Again, when he asked for food he was told about the dragon. He, too, was brave and offered to kill the dragon. The villagers were relieved and delighted.

When he arrived at the fields he also saw the giant watermelon and returned to the village to tell the villagers that they were mistaken about the dragon – they need have no fear of a giant watermelon. They hacked him to pieces.

More time passed and the villagers were becoming

desperate.

One day a third traveller appeared. He could see how desperate they were and asked what the problem was. They told him and he promised he would slay the dragon so that they could go to the fields to harvest their crops.

When he got to the field he, too, saw the giant watermelon.

He reflected for a moment, then he drew his sword, leapt into the field, and hacked the watermelon to pieces.

He returned to the villagers and told them he had killed the dragon. They were overjoyed.

The traveller stayed in the village for many months, long enough to teach the villagers the difference between dragons and watermelons.

EIGHTY NINE

The wise counsellor

In ancient Egypt there was a pharaoh who was much concerned with his own mortality.

So he called in a old and respected counsellor.

"Tell me", he said, "when do you predict that I shall die?"

The counsellor thought long and hard, and wondered how he should answer this question. How could he win the goodwill and status of the pharaoh?

A few days later he returned. "I have thought long and hard, great ruler, and I have consulted the ancient texts. I believe that you will win some great battles and not die until you have overcome your enemies."

Pleased as he was to hear this forecast, the pharaoh was not satisfied and commanded that the old man be taken away and beheaded.

But the problem was not solved and the pharaoh continued to be haunted by the prospect of his eventual death.

He asked around and was advised to consult another oracle, who was duly presented to the pharaoh.

"Tell me", he asked again, "when do you predict that I shall die?"

This new advisor had heard about the previous prediction so he tried another approach. "I predict, oh lord, that you will acquire great wealth. You will not die until you have filled your vaults with gold."

Pleased as he was to hear such a prospect foretold, the pharaoh was still not satisfied, and another advisor was despatched to his death.

So he asked around again.

This time they found him a wily young man who had recently arrived at court.

When asked the same question, he was able to reply immediately.

"Great sir, I can tell you exactly when you will die. It will be precisely three hours after my own death."

From this moment the advisor lived a charmed life!

NINETY

Think carefully before you ask

A man was contemplating his retirement when a genie appeared before him.

"What is your wish, oh master," it asked him.

"Well, I don't know. But it would be rather nice if I could have a wife who is 30 years younger than me," he replied.

"Your wish is my command. Stand by."

Suddenly, he felt stiff and tired. He looked at his body, which had become wrinkled and wasted. His joints ached, his vision was blurred.

"Whatever has happened?" he asked the genie.

"You wanted your wife to be 30 years younger than you," replied the genie. "I have made you 90 years old."

NINETY ONE

This, too, will pass

Contributed by *Deepak Lodhia*

Once upon a time, there was a great king, who recognised that the more powerful he became, the more important it was that he avoided the kind of impulsive action that can accompany both life's highs and life's lows. He tasked his council of wisdom to devise some means of reminding him that his best self lay in the middle path between laughter and tears, joy and sorrow, high and low.

Soon, they returned to him with a red-jewelled ring. Inscribed beneath the stone, the wise councillors told him, is a magical incantation. If you find yourself drunk with the giddiness of success, it will sober you up and enable you to remain wise; if you find yourself lost in the hopelessness of despair, it will bring you hope and courage.

Before the king had a chance to look beneath the stone and read the incantation, he found himself transported as if by magic to a room filled with the most beautiful women he had ever seen. The women were sirens, and as they began to sing, the king felt an overwhelming need to follow their voices at any cost. Just then, the jewel on his ring began to glow, and in its light he read for the first time the magical incantation:

This Too Will Pass

Instantly, the king regained his senses, saw the women for what they were, and turned his back on them. But no sooner had he done so than he found himself once again magically transported. This time he was seemingly trapped upon a battlefield, his men lying dead or wounded, his kingdom all but lost. Just as he was about to resign himself to his fate, the jewel on his ring once more began to glow, and he again read the incantation:

This Too Will Pass

Suddenly emboldened by hope, the king found a new strength, rallied his remaining troops, and turned the tide of the battle, saving the kingdom and all who dwelled within.

Three blind men and an elephant

One day, three blind men happened to meet each other and gossiped a long time about many things. Suddenly one of them recalled, "I heard that an elephant is a queer animal. Too bad we're blind and can't see it."

"Ah, yes, truly too bad we don't have the good fortune to see the strange animal," another one sighed.

The third one, quite annoyed, joined in and said, "See? Forget it! Just to feel it would be great."

"Well, that's true. If only there were some way of touching the elephant, we'd be able to know," they all agreed.

It so happened that a merchant with a herd of elephants was passing, and overheard their conversation. "You fellows, do you really want to feel an elephant? Then follow me; I will show you," he said.

The three men were surprised and happy. Taking one another's hand, they quickly formed a line and followed while the merchant led the way. Each one began to contemplate how he would feel the animal, and tried to figure how he would form an image.

After reaching their destination, the merchant asked them to sit on the ground to wait. In a few minutes he led the first blind man to feel the elephant. With outstretched hand, he touched first the left foreleg and then the right. After that he felt the two legs from the top to the bottom, and with a beaming face, turned to say, "So, the queer animal is just like that." Then he slowly returned to the group.

Thereupon the second blind man was led to the rear of the elephant. He touched the tail, which wagged a few times, and he exclaimed with satisfaction, "Ha! Truly a queer animal! Truly odd! I know now. I know." He hurriedly stepped aside.

The third blind man's turn came, and he touched the elephant's trunk which moved back and forth turning and twisting and he thought, "That's it! I've learned."

The three blind men thanked the merchant and went their way. Each one was secretly excited over the experience and had a lot to say, yet all walked rapidly without saying a word.

"Let's sit down and discuss this queer animal," the second blind man said, breaking the silence.

"A very good idea. Very good." the other two agreed for they also had this in mind.

Without waiting for anyone to be properly seated, the second one blurted out, "This queer animal is like our straw fans swinging back and forth to give us a breeze. However, it's not so big or well made. The main portion is rather wispy."

"No, no!" the first blind man shouted in disagreement. "This queer animal resembles two big trees without any branches."

"You're both wrong." the third man replied. "This queer animal is similar to a snake; it's long and round, and very strong."

How they argued! Each one insisted that he alone was correct.

Of course, there was no conclusion for not one had thoroughly examined the whole elephant. How can anyone describe the whole until he has learned the total of the parts.

Three coaches on a train

Three coaches were travelling on a train through the English Lake District.

As they travelled, they looked out of the window and enjoyed the beautiful countryside, including herds of black and white dairy cows.

The train continued and the passed into Scotland.

One of the coaches looked out of the window and saw three highland cattle quietly grazing. He commented, "I notice that, unlike in England, the cattle in Scotland are brown."

"Not so fast", said one of his companions, who had been taught the importance of being specific. "All that we can conclude is that three cows in Scotland are brown."

"Not at all" commented the third coach. "All that we really know is that three cattle in Scotland are brown on one side!"

NINETY FOUR

Three masons

A man was visiting a city for the first time when he noticed a large construction site.

He decided to walk across and find out what was going on and came across a group of men working with stone.

He went up to the first and asked what he was doing.

"I am breaking these rocks into building blocks. It is back breaking work but there is little other work available and at least it pays the bills."

He walked on and spoke to another man, asking him what he was doing.

"I am shaping stone from the quarry into building blocks. It is skilled work and I get great pleasure from the precision with which I am able to work. Also, I am proud to be able to provide for the needs of my family."

Walking on further, he spoke to a third worker.

"I am preparing stone blocks that will be used by the builders. We are building a great cathedral to the glory of God; it won't be finished in my lifetime but one day it will be a great asset to the city and a legacy for my grandchildren, who will be able to worship there."

NINETY FIVE

Two fish in the sea

This is a story told by Roger Hamilton

Two fish were swimming around when one of them was caught by a fisherman in a boat above.

The fisherman reeled in his line and swung the fish around to catch it in his hand.

We don't know whether the fish was too small or whether he was fishing for sport rather than food. Anyway, the fisherman unhooked the fish and threw it back into the water.

Relieved to be back home, the fish swam around looking for his friend.

"Ah, there you are", he said. "It is such a relief to be back in the water."

"What water?", replied his friend.

NINETY SIX

Two frogs in cream

This is the story of two frogs. One frog was fat and the other skinny.

One day, they were enjoying the day in the barn when they accidently fell into the farmer's bucket of cream. They couldn't get out, as the sides were too slippery, so they were just swimming around. Every once in a while they would try to climb out, but this was becoming very tiring.

The fat frog said to the skinny frog, "Brother frog, there's no use paddling any longer. We're just going to drown, so we might as well give up."

The skinny frog replied, "Hold on brother, keep paddling. Somebody will get us out." And they continued paddling for hours.

After a while, the fat frog said, "Brother frog, there's no use. I'm becoming very tired now. I'm just going to stop paddling and drown. It's Sunday and nobody's working. We're doomed. There's no possible way out of here."

But the skinny frog said, "Keep trying. Keep paddling. Something will happen, keep paddling."

Another couple of hours passed. The fat frog said, "I can't go on any longer. There's no sense in doing it because we're going to drown anyway. What's the use?" And the fat frog stopped. He gave up. And he drowned in the cream.

But the skinny frog kept on paddling.

Ten minutes later, the skinny frog felt something solid beneath his feet. He had churned the cream into butter and he hopped out of the vat.

Two monks and a damsel

Two monks were walking in the mountains, when they came to a ford. There had been rains recently and the water level had risen. A young damsel was struggling to cross.

One of the monks offered to carry her across and the girl accepted, so he picked her up and waded to the other side of the stream, where he put her down safely.

The two monks continued on their journey.

After a while, the younger monk said, "Father, I cannot believe that you carried that girl. We have taken a vow of chastity and are not allowed to touch or even think about women. And yet despite that you carried this young girl in your arms!"

The older monk looked at his brother and replied, "Yes, I did carry the girl. The difference between you and me is that I put her down when I reached the other side. You are still carrying her!"

NINETY EIGHT

Two wolves fighting

This is a Native American story

An old Cherokee is telling his granddaughter about a fight that is going on inside himself.

He said it is between two wolves.

One is evil: Anger, envy, sorrow, regret, greed, arrogance, self-pity, guilt, resentment, inferiority, lies, false pride, superiority and ego.

The other is good: Joy, peace, love, hope, serenity, humility, kindness, benevolence, empathy, generosity, truth, compassion and faith.

The granddaughter thought about it for a minute and then asked her grandfather, "Which wolf wins?"

The old Cherokee simply replied, "The one I feed."

NINETY NINE

22 ways to kill a good idea

1. Ignore it. Dead silence will intimidate all but the most enthusiastic proposers of ideas.

2. See it coming and dodge. You can recognise the imminent arrival of an idea by a growing unease and anxiety in the would be-originator. Change the subject. Or, better still, end the meeting.

3. Scorn it. The gently lifted eyebrow and a softly spoken 'You aren't really serious. Are you?' works wonders. In severe cases make the audible comment, 'Utterly impracticable'. Get your thrust home before the idea is fully explained, otherwise it might prove practicable after all.

4. Laugh it off. 'Ho, Ho, ho, that's a good one Joe. You must have sat up all night thinking that up. If he has, this makes it even funnier.

5. Praise it to death. By the time you have expounded its merits for five minutes everyone else will hate it. The proposer will be wondering what is wrong with it himself.

6. Mention that it has never been tried. If it is new this will be true.

7. Prove that it isn't new. If you can make it look

similar to a known idea, the fact that this one is better may not emerge.

8. Observe that it doesn't fit the company policy. Since nobody knows what the policy is you're probably right.

9. Mention what it will cost. The fact that the expected saving is six times as much will then pale into significance. That is imaginary money, what we spend is real. Beware of ideas that cost nothing though, and point out, 'if it doesn't cost anything, it can't be worth anything.'

10. Oh, we've tried that before. Particularly effective if the originator is a newcomer. It makes him realise what an outsider he is.

11. Cast the right aspersion. 'Isn't it a bit too flip?', or 'Do we want this clever-clever stuff?' Or 'Let's be careful we don't out smart ourselves' Such comments will draw ready applause and few ideas will survive collective disapproval.

12. Find a competitive idea. This is a dangerous one unless you are experienced, you might still get left with an idea.

13. Produce twenty good reasons why it won't work. The one good reason why it will is then lost.

14. Modify it out of existence. This is elegant; you seem to be helping the idea along, just changing a little here and there, by the time the originator wakes up it's dead.

15. Encourage doubt about ownership. Didn't you suggest something like Harry is saying 'when we first met, Jim?' While everyone is wondering, the

idea may wither and die quietly.

16. Damn it by association of ideas. Connect it with someone's pet hate. Remark casually to the Senior Man, 'Why that's just the sort of thing John might have thought up.' The senior Man loathes John. Your idea man doesn't, and will wonder for weeks what hit him.

17. Try to chip bits off it; if you fiddle with an idea long enough it might come to pieces.

18. Make a personal attack on the originator, by the time he's recovered he'll have forgotten he had an idea.

19. Score a technical knock out; for instance refer to some obscure regulation it might infringe. Use technology as a bludgeon. 'But if you're on that you'll need a pulsating oscillograph coupled with a hemispherical interferometer, so you see there should be a negative feedback on the forward rheo-stat and you wouldn't like that would you?'

20. Postpone it. By the time it's been postponed a few times it will look tatty and part worn.

21. Let a committee sit on the idea.

22. Encourage the author to look for a better idea' usually a discouraging quest. If he finds one, start him looking for a better job.

What did you see?

Extract from *Mara and Dann* by Doris Lessing

At home there was a game that all the parents played with their children. It was called, What Did You See? Mara was about Dann's age when she was first called into her father's room one evening, where he sat in his big carved and coloured chair. He said to her, 'And now we are going to play a game. What was the thing you liked best today?'

At first she chattered: 'I played with my cousin . . . I was out with Shera in the garden . . . I made a stone house.' And then he said, 'Tell me about the house.' And she said, 'I made a house out of the stones that come from the river bed.' And he said, 'Now tell me about the stones.' And she said, 'They were mostly smooth stones, but some were sharp and had different shapes.' 'Tell me what the stones looked like, what colour they were, what did they feel like.'

And by the time the game ended she knew why some stones were smooth and some sharp and why they were different colours, some cracked, some sharp and why they were almost sand. She knew how rivers rolled stones along and how some of them came from far away. She knew that the river had once been twice as wide as it was now.

There seemed no end to what she knew, and yet her

father had not told her much, but kept asking questions so she found the answers in herself. Like, 'Why do you think some stones are smooth and round and some still sharp?' And she thought and replied, 'Some have been in the water a long time, rubbing against other stones, some have only just been broken off bigger stones.'

Every evening, either her father or her mother called her in for What Did You See? She loved it. During the day, playing outside or with her toys, alone or with other children, she found herself thinking, Now notice what you are doing, so you can tell them tonight what you saw.

She had thought that the game did not change; but then one evening she was there when her little brother was first asked, What Did You See? And she knew just how much the game had changed for her. Because now it was not just What Did You See? But: What were you thinking? What made you think that? Are you sure that thought is true?

What is talent?

What is talent? "Easy to learn and easy to do."

The trouble with the skills and competences that are easy to learn and easy to do is that you probably will not value them. Indeed, you might not even recognise them.

So, how do you identify your own talent?

Notice what frustrates you in other people's apparent incompetence and foolishness. Recognise that they are probably not either incompetent or foolish. Rather, it is you who finds it easy to do.

You have discovered one of your talents.

Why are you looking there?

There is a story about someone walking along a street late at night.

He came across a man scrabbling in the gutter under a street lamp.

"What are you doing there", he asked.

"I am looking for my keys" was the reply.

"Oh dear, are you sure this is where you lost them?"

"Oh no, I lost them further along the street."

"Then why are you looking here?"

"It's dark down there and I cannot see. Here, I can see well enough to look."

USEFUL QUOTES

USEFUL QUOTES

"Ships in harbour are safe, but that's not what ships are built for." *Alan Alda*

"The best way to predict the future is to invent it." *Alan Kay*

"Imagination is more important than knowledge." *Albert Einstein*

"There are two ways to live your life. One is as though nothing is a miracle. The other is as though everything is a miracle." *Albert Einstein*

"There are people who, instead of listening to what is being said to them, are already listening to what they are going to say themselves." *Albert Guinon*

"If I weren't so busy, I'd get really excited!" Andy Middleton

"You can't have a plan for your day until you have a plan for your life." *Anthony Robbins*

"When you're green you grow; when you're ripe you rot." *Anthony Robbins*

"Excellence is not an act but a habit that we repeatedly do." *Aristotle*

"You must be the change you wish to see in the world." Mahatma Ghandi

"Become a dynamo of irrepressible joy." *Babaji*

"I do not seek to follow in the footsteps of the men of

old; I seek the things they sought." Basho

"Perfection can be a fetish" *Bernard Leach*

"I don't know the key to success, but the key to failure is trying to please everybody."*Bill Cosby*

"Children are our elders in Universe time." Buckminster Fuller

"There is nothing about a caterpillar that tells you it's going to be a butterfly." *Buckminster Fuller*

"The minute you begin to do what you want to do, it's a different kind of life." *Buckminster Fuller*

"There are two mistakes you can make along the road to truth — not going all the way, and not starting." *Buddha*

"No man ever listened himself out of a job." *Calvin Coolidge*

"If grass can grow through concrete, then love can find you at any time in your life." *Cher*

"We are all motivated by a keen desire for praise, and the better a man is, the more he is inspired by glory." *Cicero*

"How many cares one loses when one decides not to be something, but to be someone." *Coco Chanel*

"Remember that not getting what you want is sometimes a wonderful stroke of luck." *Dalai Lama*

"There is always room at the top." *Daniel Webster*

"Small opportunities are often the beginning of great enterprises." *Demosthenes*

"Until you make peace with who you are, you will never be content with what you have." *Doris Mortman*

"The Universe is full of magical things patiently waiting for our wits to grow sharper." *E. Pillpotts*

"Life is the dancer and you are the dance." *Echkart Tolle*

"What is life, without a dream?" *Edmund Rostand*

"God will not look you over for medals, degrees, or diplomas, but for scars." *Elbert Hubbard*

"Learn from the mistakes of others. You can't live long enough to make them all yourself. " *Eleanor Roosevelt*

"What could we accomplish if we knew we could not fail?" *Eleanor Roosevelt*

"Do one thing every day that scares you." *Eleanor Roosevelt*

"Every day, in every way, I am getting better and better." *Emile Coue*

"When people talk, listen completely. Most people never listen." *Ernest Hemingway*

"You cannot discover new oceans unless you have the courage to lose sight of the shore." *Francis Drake*

"To listen closely and reply well is the highest perfection we are able to attain in the art of conversation." *Francois de La Rochefoucauld*

"Be a good listener. Your ears will never get you in trouble." *Frank Tyger*

"The world will never starve for want of wonders, but

only for want of wonder." *G. K. Chesterton*

"If you just set people in motion, they'll heal themselves." *Gabrielle Roth*

"Success is how high you bounce when you hit the bottom." *General George S Paton*

"I want to be thoroughly used up when I die, for the harder I work the more I live. I rejoice in life lived for its own sake. Life is no "brief candle" to me. It is a sort of splendid torch which I have got hold of for the moment, and I want to make it burn as brightly as possible before handing it on to future generations." *George Bernard Shaw*

"Both optimists and pessimists contribute to the society. The optimist invents the aeroplane, the pessimist the parachute." *George Bernard Shaw*

"It's never too late to become what you might have been." *George Eliot*

"How simple it is to see that we can only be happy now, and there will never be a time when it is not now." *Gerald Jampolsky*

"Whatever you can do or dream you can do, begin it. Boldness has genius, power and magic in it. Begin it now." *Goethe*

"Things that matter most must never be at the mercy of things that matter least." *Goethe*

"Each morning when I open my eyes I say to myself: "I, not events, have the power to make me happy or unhappy today. I can choose which it shall be. Yesterday is dead, tomorrow hasn't arrived yet. I have just one day, today, and I'm going to be happy in it." *Groucho Marx*

"That which we persist in doing becomes easier to do, not that the nature of the thing has changed, but our power to do so is increased." *Heber J. Grant*

"Don't find fault find a remedy." *Henry Ford*

"Quality means doing it right when on one is looking." *Henry Ford*

"This company doesn't pay anybody. Only customers can do that. The company merely handles the money." *Henry Ford*

"Nothing is so fatiguing as the hanging on of an uncompleted task." *Henry James*

"If you ask managers what they do, they will most likely tell you that they plan, organise, co-ordinate and control. Then watch what they do. Don't be surprised if you can't relate what you see to those four words." *Henry Mintzberg*

"If you do not expect the unexpected you will not find it, for it is not to be reached by search or trial." *Heraclitus*

"Adversity reveals genius, prosperity conceals it." *Horace*

"Remember when life's path is steep to keep your mind even." *Horace*

"Life is like a game of cards. The hand that is dealt you represents determinism; the way you play it is free will." *Jawaharlal Nehru*

"One is still what one is going to cease to be and already

what one is going to become." *Jean Paul Sartre*

"Life is what happens to you while you are busy making other plans." *John Lennon*

"Your dreams tell you what to do; your reason tells you how to do it." *Jonas Salk*

"May you live all the days of your life." *Jonathan Swift*

"He who has imagination without learning has wings and no feet." *Joseph Joubert*

"There is no expedient to which a man will not resort to avoid the real labour of thinking." *Sir Joshua Reynolds*

"If you obey all the rules, you miss all the fun." *Katherine Hepburn*

"You don't have to be great to get started, but you have to get started to be great." *Les Brown*

"You only live once but, if you do it right, once is enough." *Mae West*

"A career is wonderful, but you can't curl up with a career on a cold night!" *Marilyn Munro*

"Twenty years from now, you will be more disappointed by the things that you didn't do than by the ones you did do. So throw off the bowlines. Sail away from the safe harbour. Catch the trade winds in your sails. Explore. Dream. Discover." *Mark Twain*

"Take the first step in faith. You don't have to see the whole staircase, just take the first step." *Martin Luther King*

"A computer lets you make more mistakes faster than any other invention in human history, with the possible exception of handguns and tequila." *Mitch Radcliffe*

"If you judge people, you have no time to love them." *Mother Theresa*

"Be kind and merciful. Let no one ever come to you without coming away better and happier." *Mother Theresa*

"If one can't be happy, one must be amused...." *Nancy Mitford*

"A man who wants to lead the orchestra must turn his back on the crowd." *Ninon de Vere de Rosa*

"I'll never forget what's his name." *Norman Pliscou*

"Beginning today, treat everyone you meet as if he or she were going to be dead by midnight. Extend to them all the care, kindness, and understanding you can muster, and do so with no thought of any reward. Your life will never be the same again." *Og Mandino*

"Man's mind, once stretched by a new idea, never regains its original dimensions." *Oliver Wendell Holmes*

"A blind man who sees is better than a seeing man who is blind." Persian proverb

"We will not have failure – only success and new learning." *Queen Victoria*

"What lies behind us and what lies before us are small matters compared to what lies within us." *Ralph Waldo Emerson*

"Our chief want in life is somebody who will make us do what we can." *Ralph Waldo Emerson*

"If you care about what people think about you, how will you ever know how you feel about you?" *Rebecca Fisher*

"I am poor and naked, but I am the chief of the nation. We do not want riches but we do want to train our children right. Riches would do us no good. We could not take them with us to the other world. We do not want riches. We want peace and love." *Red Cloud, Sioux Chief*

"God grant me the serenity to accept things I cannot change, the courage to change the things I can, and the wisdom to know the difference." *Reinhold Niebuhr*

"You are never given a wish without also being given the power to make it true." *Richard Bach*

"Dreamers only dream, but creators bring their dreams into reality." *Robert Fritz*

"The longer the excuse, the less likely it's the truth." *Robert Half*

"I know that you believe you understand what you think I said, but I'm not sure you realise that what you heard is not what I meant." *Robert McCloskey*

"The key to happiness — is an ability to celebrate the ordinary." *Roy H Williams*

"Nothing at all will be attempted if all possible objections must first be overcome." *Samuel Johnson*

"Employ your time in improving yourself by other people's writings, so that you shall gain easily what others have laboured hard for." *Socrates*

"Look after your laundry, and your soul will look after itself." *Somerset Maugham*

"It is a funny thing about life; if you refuse to accept anything but the best, you very often get it." *Somerset Maugham*

"An empowered organisation is one in which individuals have the knowledge, skill, desire, and opportunity to personally succeed in a way that leads to collective organisational success." *Stephen R. Covey*

The worst enemy to creativity is self doubt. *Sylvia Plath*

"Only those who risk going too far can possibly find out how far they can go." *T S Eliot*

"You will find that you survive humiliation. And that's an experience of incalculable value." *T S Eliot*

"Your heart will give you greater teachings than all the world's scholars." *The Talmud*

"If we did all the things we are capable of doing, we would literally astound ourselves." *Thomas Edison*

"Perhaps the most valuable result of all education is the ability to make yourself do the thing you have to do, when it ought to be done, whether you like it or not." *Thomas Huxley*

"It is difficult to get a man to understand something when his salary depends upon his not understanding it." *Upton Sinclair*

"The vision must be followed by the venture. It is not

enough to stare up the steps - we must step up the stairs." *Vance Havner*

"There is one thing stronger than all the armies in the world, and that is an idea whose time has come." *Victor Hugo*

"The quality of a person's life is in direct proportion to their commitment to excellence, regardless of endeavour." *Vincent T Lombardi*

"It's kind of fun to do the impossible." *Walt Disney*

"We can choose to make our love for each other what our lives are really about." *Werner Erhard*

"As a man is, so he sees." *William Blake*

"The secret of a man how is universally interesting is that he is universally interested." *William Dean Howells*

"People are where they are because that's exactly where they really want to be... whether they'll admit that or not." *William James*

"Dance like no one is watching, Love like you'll never be hurt, Sing like no one is listening, Live like it's heaven on earth." *William Purkey*

"Personally, I'm always ready to learn, although I do not always like being taught." *Winston Churchill*

"I am easily satisfied with the very best." *Winston Churchill*

"The price of greatness is responsibility." *Winston Churchill*

"You already have every characteristic necessary for success if you recognize, claim, develop and use them."
Zig Ziglar

Bonus quotations

"Have less, do less, be more!"

"Practise random kindness and senseless acts of beauty."

"Joy is peace dancing, peace is joy resting."

"Life is too short to learn only from my own mistakes."

"Turn your face to the sun and the shadows will fall behind you."

"The instructions for thinking outside the box are printed on the outside."

"Usually, the brain that contains the problem is the brain that contains the solution."

When smart people get together good things happen.

POEMS

POEMS

If

Rudyard Kipling

If you can keep your head when all about you
Are losing theirs and blaming it on you,
If you can trust yourself when all men doubt you,
But make allowance for their doubting too;

If you can wait and not be tired by waiting,
Or being lied about, don't deal in lies,
Or being hated, don't give way to hating,
And yet don't look too good, nor talk too wise:

If you can dream - and not make dreams your
  master,
If you can think - and not make thoughts your
  aim;
If you can meet with Triumph and Disaster
And treat those two impostors just the same;

If you can bear to hear the truth you've spoken
Twisted by knaves to make a trap for fools,
Or watch the things you gave your life to, broken,

And stoop and build 'em up with worn-out tools:

If you can make one heap of all your winnings
And risk it all on one turn of pitch-and-toss,
And lose, and start again at your beginnings
And never breath a word about your loss;

If you can force your heart and nerve and sinew
To serve your turn long after they are gone,
And so hold on when there is nothing in you
Except the Will which says to them: "Hold on!"

If you can talk with crowds and keep your virtue,
Or walk with kings - nor lose the common touch,
If neither foes nor loving friends can hurt you,
If all men count with you, but none too much;

If you can fill the unforgiving minute
With sixty seconds' worth of distance run,
Yours is the Earth and everything that's in it,
And - which is more - you'll be a Man, my son!

Leaders

Leaders are best when people scarcely know they exist

Not so good when people obey and acclaim them

Worst when people despise them.

Fail to honour people, they fail to honour you.

But of good leaders, who talk little,

when their work is done, task fulfilled,

people will say: "We have done this ourselves!"

Verse 17 Tao Te Ching

Listen

This poem is un-attributed but it is understood to have been written during the 30 year period that the author was held in a mental institution. It speaks volumes about the need for us to change the way in which we treat our fellow human beings.

When I ask you to listen to me, and you start giving me advice,
You have not done what I asked.

When I ask you to listen to me and you begin to
tell me why I shouldn't feel that way,
You are trampling on my feelings.

When I ask you to listen to me and you feel you
have to do something to solve my problems,
You have failed me, strange as that may seem.

Listen! All I ask is that you listen; not talk, nor do
— just hear me.

And I can do for myself "I'm not helpless.
Maybe discouraged and faltering, but not helpless.

When you do something for me, that I can and

need to do for myself,
You contribute to my fear and weakness.

But when you accept as a simple fact that I do feel
what I feel, no matter how irrational
then I quit trying to convince you and can get
about the business of understanding what's behind
this irrational feeling.

When that's clear, the answers are obvious and I
don't need advice.
Irrational feelings make sense when we understand
what's behind them.

Perhaps that's why prayer works sometimes for
some people;
Because God is mute and does not give advice to
try to "fix" things, He/She just listens, and lets you
work it out for yourself.

So please listen, and just hear me, and if you want
to talk,
wait a minute for your turn, and I'll listen to you.

POEMS

Navajo Chant

When you were born
You cried
And the world rejoiced.

Live your life so that
When you die
The world cries and you rejoice.

Our Deepest Fear

Marianne Williamson

Our deepest fear is not that we are inadequate.
Our deepest fear is that we are powerful beyond
measure.
It is our light, not our darkness
That most frightens us.

We ask ourselves
Who am I to be brilliant, gorgeous, talented,
fabulous?
Actually, who are you not to be?
You are a child of God.

Your playing small
Does not serve the world.
There's nothing enlightened about shrinking
So that other people won't feel insecure around
you.

We are all meant to shine,
As children do.
We were born to make manifest
The glory of God that is within us.

It's not just in some of us;
It's in everyone.

And as we let our own light shine,
We unconsciously give other people permission
to do the same.
As we're liberated from our own fear,
Our presence automatically liberates others.

POEMS

Six honest serving men

Rudyard Kipling

> I keep six honest serving men.
> (They taught me all I knew);
> Their names are What and Why and When
> And How and Where and Who.

POEMS

The parable of the cautious man

There was a very cautious man
who never laughed or cried.
He never risked, he never lost,
he never won, nor tried.

And when he one day passed away,
his insurance was denied.
For since he never really lived,
they claimed he never died!

POEMS

The Stress-free Workplace in 50 years time

A poem written by pupils at Leechpool Lane School for Roffey Park Management Institute (in 1996)

> The stress-free workplace,
> It really could be true.
> Work and pleasure rolled into one.
> Read on, this could be you.
>
> The main building is the workplace
> The rest is to unwind.
> The gym, the sauna, a restaurant,
> Are pictures in my mind.
>
> The gym a place to workout
> Or badminton if you care,
> A peace garden to wander round
> No noise or hassle there.
>
> A music area to express your thought
> Or to calm any tension.
> What a place this really is,
> I could work there 'till my pension.

A creche to cater for the tiny tots
Their every need provided.
While you go off and do your work
In caring hands they're guided.

A restaurant to serve delicious meals
Or even just a snack.
A bar for drinks or to tell a joke,
There's nothing here we lack.

A conference room to discuss and plan.
A table with many places,
A lecture room to learn things new,
A theatre full of faces.

The stress free workplace,
It really could be true.
The idea of this is possible.
Your future's here, are you?

Thought

D H Lawrence

Thought, I love thought.

But not the juggling and twisting of already exis-
tent ideas.

I despise that self-important game.

Thought is the welling up of unknown life into
consciousness,

Thought is the testing of statements on the
touchstone of consciousness,

Thought is gazing onto the face of life, and reading what can be read,

Thought is pondering over experience, and coming to conclusion.

Thought is not a trick, or an exercise, or a set of
dodges,

Thought is a man in his wholeness, wholly at-
tending.

To everything there is a season

This concept was first described in the book of Ecclesiastes, and traditionally ascribed to King Solomon.

Pete Seeger took the words and turned them into a song 'Turn! Turn! Turn!'.

"To every thing there is a season, and a time to every purpose under the heaven:

A time to be born, and a time to die; a time to plant, a time to reap that which is planted;

A time to kill, and a time to heal; a time to break down, and a time to build up;

A time to weep, and a time to laugh; a time to mourn, and a time to dance;

A time to cast away stones, and a time to gather stones together; a time to embrace, and a time to refrain from embracing;

A time to get, and a time to lose; a time to keep, and a time to cast away;

A time to rend, and a time to sew; a time to keep silence, and a time to speak;

A time to love, and a time to hate; a time of war, and a time of peace."

APPENDIX

The appendix contains longer stories; either classic stories or a full description of the facts behind the simple version of the story that is usually used in training.

Acres of Diamonds

This is from a famous speech by Russell Conwell.

"The old guide told me that there once lived not far from the River Indus an ancient Persian by the name of Ali Hafed. He said that Ali Hafed owned a very large farm; that he had orchards, grain-fields, and gardens; that he had money at interest and was a wealthy and contented man. One day there visited that old Persian farmer one of those ancient Buddhist priests, one of the wise men of the East. He sat down by the fire and told the old farmer how this old world of ours was made.

He said that this world was once a mere bank of fog, and that the Almighty thrust His finger into this bank of fog, and began slowly to move His finger around, increasing the speed until at last He whirled this bank of fog into a solid ball of fire. Then it went rolling through the universe, burning its way through other banks of fog, and condensed the moisture without, until it fell in floods of rain upon its hot surface, and cooled the outward crust. Then the internal fires bursting outward through the crust threw up the mountains and hills, the valleys, the plains and prairies of this wonderful world of ours. If this internal molten mass came bursting out and cooled very quickly, it became granite; less quickly copper, less quickly silver, less quickly gold, and, after gold, diamonds were made. Said the old priest, "A diamond is a congealed drop of sunlight." Now that is literally scientifically true, that a diamond is an actual deposit of carbon from the sun.

The old priest told Ali Hafed that if he had one diamond the size of his thumb he could purchase the county, and if the had a mine of diamonds he could place his children upon thrones through the influence of their great wealth. Ali Hafed heard all about diamonds, how much they were worth, and went to his bed that night a poor man. He had not lost anything, but he was poor because he was discontented, and discontented because he feared he was poor. He said, "I want a mine of diamonds," and he lay awake all night. Early in the morning he sought out the priest. I know by experience that a priest is very cross when awakened early in the morning, and when he shook that old priest out of his dreams, Ali Hafed said to him:

"Will you tell me where I find diamonds?"

"Diamonds! What do you want with diamonds?"

"Why, I wish to be immensely rich."

"Well, then, go along and find them. That is all you have to do; go and find them, and then you have them."

"But I don't know where to go."

"Well, if you will find a river that runs through white sands, between high mountains, in those white sands you will always find diamonds."

"I don't believe there is any such river."

"Oh yes, there are plenty of them. All you have to do is to go and find them, and then you have them."

Said Ali Hafed, "I will go."

So he sold his farm, collected his money, left his family in charge of a neighbour, and away he went in search of diamonds. He began his search, very properly to my mind, at the Mountains of the Moon. Afterward he came around into Palestine, then wandered on into Europe, and at last when his money was all spent and he was in rags, wretchedness, and poverty, he stood on the shore of that bay at Barcelona, in Spain, when a great tidal wave came rolling in between the pillars of Hercules, and the poor, afflicted, suffering, dying man could not resist the awful temptation to cast himself into that incoming tide, and he sank beneath its foaming crest, never to rise in this life again.

Then after that old guide had told me that awfully sad story, he stopped the camel I was riding on and went back to fix the baggage that was coming off another camel, and I had an opportunity to muse over his story while he was gone. I remember saying to myself, "Why did he reserve that story for his 'particular friends'?" There seemed to be no beginning, no middle, no end, nothing to it.

That was the first story I had ever heard told in my life, and would be the first one I ever read, in which the hero was killed in the first chapter. I had but one chapter of that story, and the hero was dead. When the guide came back and took up the halter of my camel, he went right ahead with the story, into the second chapter, just as though there had been no break.

The man who purchased Ali Hafed's farm one day led his camel into the garden to drink, and as that camel put its nose into the shallow water of that garden brook, Ali Hafed's successor noticed a curious flash of light from the white sands of the stream. He pulled out a black stone having an eye of light reflecting all the hues of the rainbow. He took the pebble into the house and put it on the mantel which covers the central fires, and forgot all about it.

A few days later this same old priest came in to visit Ali Hafed's successor, and the moment he opened that drawing-room door he saw that flash of light on the mantel, and he rushed up to it, and shouted:

"Here is a diamond! Has Ali Hafed returned?"

"Oh no, Ali Hafed has not returned, and that is not a diamond. That is nothing but a stone we found right out here in our own garden."

"But," said the priest, "I tell you I know a diamond when I see it. I know positively that is a diamond."

Then together they rushed out into that old garden and stirred up the white sands with their fingers, and lo! There came up other more beautiful and valuable gems than the first. "Thus," said the guide to me, "was discovered the diamond-mine of Golconda, the most magnificent diamond-mine in all the history of mankind, excelling the Kimberly itself. The Kohinoor, and the Orloff of the crown jewels of England and Russia, the largest on earth, came from that mine."

Michelangelo's David

Michelangelo's David is worked from an enormous block of marble; it weighs six tonnes and is five metres high.

Michelangelo is often quoted by trainers looking for a metaphor.

"In every block of marble I see a statue as plain as though it stood before me, shaped and perfect in attitude and action. I have only to hew away the rough walls that imprison the lovely apparition to reveal it to the other eyes as mine see it."

However, there are more aspects to the story from which lessons can be drawn.

The block of Tuscan marble used for the statue had confounded great sculptors decades before Michelangelo even picked up his chisel.

During the 1460s sculptors had been unable to cope with the size of the block because it was too big.

At the beginning of the 16th century the idea was resurrected and the young Michelangelo sensed an opportunity. He managed to carve the whole statue in less than two years, even though he was famous for not finishing things.

Given that he was an artist in his mid-20s with few high-profile pieces in his portfolio, this was a major step.

The sculpture was inspired by the Bible story of the young shepherd boy who chose to fight a far stronger adversary in order to save his people from invasion. Wearing no armour, with a sling as his only weapon, David defeats Goliath using superior skill and courage.

Michelangelo shows David not as a triumphant victor, but as a thinking, resolute being — the preconditions for victory.

Although there had been many earlier portrayals of David in art, Michelangelo's was revolutionary. The others depict David after the battle had been won — often standing on the severed head of a defeated Goliath. Michelangelo chose to show David not in victory, but at that point in time that prefigured victory: in that instance between conscious choice and conscious action, that moment when an individual makes a choice — and commits to act on that choice. David stands, with furrowed brow, looking over his left shoulder into the distance for Goliath.

Michelangelo had heard about a big block of marble eighteen feet high that was sitting around in a yard. He went to the town hall to ask about it and was told that the mayor had promised it to a sculptor called Sansovino. Another official said he had heard it was meant for Leonardo da Vinci. In any case, the best thing would be for Michelangelo to forget about it because it was worthless.

"Didn't they tell you?" said the official. "A fellow called Simone da Fiesole started to carve a statue years ago and the fool began by drilling a big hole right through the block. If it had been a clean hole maybe something could still be done; but then the guy goes and chips half the stone away from front and back of the hole too. A dozen sculptors have gone to look at it and they all come back here either angry or nearly crying. It was a beautiful block too, without any flaws. Da Fiesole ought to be hanged."

Michelangelo knew the story and he had often wondered just how bad the botch was and whether he could cut a figure out of that block, hole and all. That a dozen other sculptors hadn't been able to do so didn't mean a thing to him, so he asked to be allowed to go and see it.

In the yard of the Office of Works Michelangelo spent a long time at the stone. He walked around it, took measurements, stood in front of it in thought.

"Now you see for yourself why everyone else rejected the darn thing," said the old caretaker with all the keys; but he got no answer from Michelangelo.

As soon as he was home Michelangelo started drawing and making a little wax model of a David, which had been da Fiesole's subject. When he was sure he could carve his figure out of the botched block, he asked the mayor, Soderini, to give it to him.

He carved the David, according to Condivi, though few believe this, in eighteen months and "extracted the statue so exactly that the old rough surface of the marble [and da Fiesole's chisel marks] still appear on the top of the head and on the base."

As he was finishing the statue Piero Soderini who was the Gonfaloniere (one of the highest posts in the Florentine government) stopped by and said that he really liked the David but that the nose was too big and that Michelangelo should chisel it down to make it smaller. Michelangelo had no intention of changing the finished David but also thought that Soderini was looking at it from the wrong angle. He climbed a ladder with a handful of marble dust and his chisel and pretended to chisel as he threw the dust around.

When he asked him what he thought now Soderini said, "I like it better, you've made it come alive."

St. Crispen's Day Speech

Henry V, by William Shakespeare

WESTMORELAND. O that we now had here
But one ten thousand of those men in England
That do no work to-day!

KING. What's he that wishes so?
My cousin Westmoreland? No, my fair cousin;
If we are mark'd to die, we are enow
To do our country loss; and if to live,
The fewer men, the greater share of honour.
God's will! I pray thee, wish not one man more.
By Jove, I am not covetous for gold,
Nor care I who doth feed upon my cost;
It yearns me not if men my garments wear;
Such outward things dwell not in my desires.
But if it be a sin to covet honour,
I am the most offending soul alive.
No, faith, my coz, wish not a man from England.
God's peace! I would not lose so great an honour

As one man more methinks would share from me
For the best hope I have. O, do not wish one more!
Rather proclaim it, Westmoreland, through my host,
That he which hath no stomach to this fight,
Let him depart; his passport shall be made,
And crowns for convoy put into his purse;
We would not die in that man's company
That fears his fellowship to die with us.
This day is call'd the feast of Crispian.
He that outlives this day, and comes safe home,
Will stand a tip-toe when this day is nam'd,
And rouse him at the name of Crispian.
He that shall live this day, and see old age,
Will yearly on the vigil feast his neighbours,
And say 'To-morrow is Saint Crispian.'
Then will he strip his sleeve and show his scars,
And say 'These wounds I had on Crispian's day.'
Old men forget; yet all shall be forgot,
But he'll remember, with advantages,
What feats he did that day. Then shall our names,
Familiar in his mouth as household words-
Harry the King, Bedford and Exeter,
Warwick and Talbot, Salisbury and Gloucester-
Be in their flowing cups freshly rememb'red.
This story shall the good man teach his son;
And Crispin Crispian shall ne'er go by,

From this day to the ending of the world,
But we in it shall be remembered-
We few, we happy few, we band of brothers;
For he to-day that sheds his blood with me
Shall be my brother; be he ne'er so vile,
This day shall gentle his condition;
And gentlemen in England now-a-bed
Shall think themselves accurs'd they were not here,
And hold their manhoods cheap whiles any speaks
That fought with us upon Saint Crispin's day.

Stanford Commencement Address

Delivered by Steve Jobs on June 12, 2005.

I am honoured to be with you today at your commencement from one of the finest universities in the world. I never graduated from college. Truth be told, this is the closest I've ever gotten to a college graduation. Today I want to tell you three stories from my life. That's it. No big deal. Just three stories.

The first story is about connecting the dots.

I dropped out of Reed College after the first 6 months, but then stayed around as a drop-in for another 18 months or so before I really quit. So why did I drop out?

It started before I was born. My biological mother was a young, unwed college graduate student, and she decided to put me up for adoption. She felt very strongly that I should be adopted by college graduates, so everything was all set for me to be adopted at birth by a lawyer and his wife. Except that when I popped out they decided at the last minute that they really wanted a girl. So my parents, who were on a waiting list, got a call in the middle of the night asking: "We have an unexpected baby boy; do you want him?" They said: "Of course." My biological mother later found out that my mother had never graduated from college and that my father had never graduated from high school. She refused to sign the final adoption papers. She only relented a few months later when my parents promised that I would someday go to college.

And 17 years later I did go to college. But I naively chose a college that was almost as expensive as Stanford, and all of my working-class parents' savings were being spent on my college tuition. After six months, I couldn't see the value in it. I had no idea what I wanted to do with my life and no idea how college was going to help me figure it out. And here I was spending all of the money my parents had saved their entire life. So I decided to drop out and trust that it would all work out OK. It was pretty scary at the time, but looking back it was one of the best decisions I ever made. The minute I dropped out I could stop taking the required classes that didn't interest me, and begin dropping in on the ones that looked interesting.

It wasn't all romantic. I didn't have a dorm room, so I slept on the floor in friends' rooms, I returned coke bottles for the 5¢ deposits to buy food with, and I would walk the 7 miles across town every Sunday night to get one good meal a week at the Hare Krishna temple. I loved it. And much of what I stumbled into by following my curiosity and intuition turned out to be priceless later on. Let me give you one example:

Reed College at that time offered perhaps the best calligraphy instruction in the country. Throughout the campus every poster, every label on every drawer, was beautifully hand calligraphed. Because I had dropped out and didn't have to take the normal classes, I decided to take a calligraphy class to learn how to do this. I learned about serif and san serif typefaces, about varying the amount of space between different letter combinations, about what makes great typography great. It was beautiful, historical, artistically subtle in a way that science can't capture, and I found it fascinating.

None of this had even a hope of any practical application in my life. But ten years later, when we were designing the first Macintosh computer, it all came back to me. And we designed it all into the Mac. It was the first computer with beautiful typography. If I had never dropped in on that single course in college, the Mac would have never had multiple typefaces or proportionally spaced fonts. And since Windows just copied the Mac, it's likely that no personal computer would have them. If I had never dropped out, I would have never dropped in on this calligraphy class, and personal computers might not have the wonderful typography that they do. Of course it was impossible to connect the dots looking forward when I was in college. But it was very, very clear looking backwards ten years later.

Again, you can't connect the dots looking forward; you can only connect them looking backwards. So you have to trust that the dots will somehow connect in your future. You have to trust in something — your gut, destiny, life, karma, whatever. This approach has never let me down, and it has made all the difference in my life.

My second story is about love and loss.

I was lucky — I found what I loved to do early in life. Woz and I started Apple in my parents garage when I was 20. We worked hard, and in 10 years Apple had grown from just the two of us in a garage into a $2 billion company with over 4000 employees. We had just released our finest creation — the Macintosh — a year earlier, and I had just turned 30. And then I got fired. How can you get fired from a company you started? Well, as Apple grew we hired someone who I thought was very talented to run the company with me, and for the first year or so things went well. But then our visions of the future began to diverge and eventually we had a falling out. When we did, our Board of Directors sided with him. So at 30 I was out. And very publicly out. What had been the focus of my entire adult life was gone, and it was devastating.

I really didn't know what to do for a few months. I felt that I had let the previous generation of entrepreneurs down - that I had dropped the baton as it was being passed to me. I met with David Packard and Bob Noyce and tried to apologise for screwing up so badly. I was a very public failure, and I even thought about running away from the valley. But something slowly began to dawn on me — I still loved what I did. The turn of events at Apple had not changed that one bit. I had been rejected, but I was still in love. And so I decided to start over.

I didn't see it then, but it turned out that getting fired from Apple was the best thing that could have ever happened to me. The heaviness of being successful was replaced by the lightness of being a beginner again, less sure about everything. It freed me to enter one of the most creative periods of my life.

During the next five years, I started a company named NeXT, another company named Pixar, and fell in love with an amazing woman who would become my wife. Pixar went on to create the worlds first computer animated feature film, Toy Story, and is now the most successful animation studio in the world. In a remarkable turn of events, Apple bought NeXT, I returned to Apple, and the technology we developed at NeXT is at the heart of Apple's current renaissance. And Laurene and I have a wonderful family together.

I'm pretty sure none of this would have happened if I hadn't been fired from Apple. It was awful tasting medicine, but I guess the patient needed it. Sometimes life hits you in the head with a brick. Don't lose faith. I'm convinced that the only thing that kept me going was that I loved what I did. You've got to find what you love. And that is as true for your work as it is for your lovers. Your work is going to fill a large part of your life, and the only way to be truly satisfied is to do what you believe is great work. And the only way to do great work is to love what you do. If you haven't found it yet, keep looking. Don't settle. As with all matters of the heart, you'll know when you find it. And, like any great relationship, it just gets better and better as the years roll on. So keep looking until you find it. Don't settle.

My third story is about death.

When I was 17, I read a quote that went something like: "If you live each day as if it was your last, someday you'll most certainly be right." It made an impression on me, and since then, for the past 33 years, I have looked in the mirror every morning and asked myself: "If today were the last day of my life, would I want to do what I am about to do today?" And whenever the answer has been "No" for too many days in a row, I know I need to change something.

Remembering that I'll be dead soon is the most important tool I've ever encountered to help me make the big choices in life. Because almost everything — all external expectations, all pride, all fear of embarrassment or failure - these things just fall away in the face of death, leaving only what is truly important. Remembering that you are going to die is the best way I know to avoid the trap of thinking you have something to lose. You are already naked. There is no reason not to follow your heart.

About a year ago I was diagnosed with cancer. I had a scan at 7:30 in the morning, and it clearly showed a tumour on my pancreas. I didn't even know what a pancreas was. The doctors told me this was almost certainly a type of cancer that is incurable, and that I should expect to live no longer than three to six months. My doctor advised me to go home and get my affairs in order, which is doctor's code for prepare to die. It means to try to tell your kids everything you thought you'd have the next 10 years to tell them in just a few months. It means to make sure everything is buttoned up so that it will be as easy as possible for your family. It means to say your goodbyes.

I lived with that diagnosis all day. Later that evening I had a biopsy, where they stuck an endoscope down my throat, through my stomach and into my intestines, put a needle into my pancreas and got a few cells from the tumour. I was sedated, but my wife, who was there, told me that when they viewed the cells under a microscope the doctors started crying because it turned out to be a very rare form of pancreatic cancer that is curable with surgery. I had the surgery and I'm fine now.

This was the closest I've been to facing death, and I hope it's the closest I get for a few more decades. Having lived through it, I can now say this to you with a bit more certainty than when death was a useful but purely intellectual concept:

No one wants to die. Even people who want to go to heaven don't want to die to get there. And yet death is the destination we all share. No one has ever escaped it. And that is as it should be, because Death is very likely the single best invention of Life. It is Life's change agent. It clears out the old to make way for the new. Right now the new is you, but someday not too long from now, you will gradually become the old and be cleared away. Sorry to be so dramatic, but it is quite true.

Your time is limited, so don't waste it living someone else's life. Don't be trapped by dogma — which is living with the results of other people's thinking. Don't let the noise of others' opinions drown out your own inner voice. And most important, have the courage to follow your heart and intuition. They somehow already know what you truly want to become. Everything else is secondary.

When I was young, there was an amazing publication called The Whole Earth Catalog, which was one of the bibles of my generation. It was created by a fellow named Stewart Brand not far from here in Menlo Park, and he brought it to life with his poetic touch. This was in the late 1960's, before personal computers and desktop publishing, so it was all made with typewriters, scissors, and polaroid cameras. It was sort of like Google in paperback form, 35 years before Google came along: it was idealistic, and overflowing with neat tools and great notions.

Stewart and his team put out several issues of The Whole Earth Catalog, and then when it had run its course, they put out a final issue. It was the mid-1970s, and I was your age. On the back cover of their final issue was a photograph of an early morning country road, the kind you might find yourself hitchhiking on if you were so adventurous. Beneath it were the words: "Stay Hungry. Stay Foolish." It was their farewell message as they signed off. Stay Hungry. Stay Foolish. And I have always wished that for myself. And now, as you graduate to begin anew, I wish that for you.

Stay Hungry. Stay Foolish.

Thank you all very much.

The marshmallow test

During the 1960s, psychologist Walter Mischel conducted what has since become known as the "marshmallow test" with four-year-olds, including his own children Carolyn and Craig, at Bing Nursery School on the campus of Stanford University, to assess each preschooler's ability to delay gratification.

Each four-year-old was given one marshmallow. They were told that they could eat it immediately or, if they waited until the researcher returned in 20 minutes, they could have two marshmallows.

If they rang a bell in the meantime, the researcher would come running back and they could eat one marshmallow but would forfeit the second. The researcher then left the room.

Some children in the group just couldn't wait. They gobbled down the marshmallow immediately.

The rest struggled hard to resist eating it. They covered their eyes, talked to themselves, sang, played games, and even tried to go to sleep.

As promised, the preschoolers who were able to wait were rewarded with two marshmallows when the researcher returned.

Carolyn had no difficulty delaying her gratification but Craig, a year older than Carolyn, was one of those who displayed less fortitude. At a certain point he realised that he was alone and started to help himself to all the candy.

Most children were like Craig; they struggled to resist the treat and held out on average for less than three minutes. Many didn't even bother ringing the bell. Others would stare directly at the marshmallow and then ring the bell thirty seconds later.

About thirty per cent of the children were like Carolyn. They successfully delayed gratification until the researcher returned, some fifteen minutes later. They wrestled with temptation but found a way to resist.

After publishing a few papers about the study, Mischel moved on to other things. But he would occasionally ask his children about their friends from nursery school. As time moved on, he began to notice a link between the children's academic performance as teenagers and their ability to await the second marshmallow.

As a result he sent out a questionnaire to all the reachable parents, teachers and academic advisers of the 653 subjects who had participated in the original marshmallow experiments. He asked about their capacity to plan and think ahead, cope well with problems and get along with their peers.

The differences were significant. Those who had been able to control their impulses and delay gratification as four-year-olds, were more effective socially and personally. They had higher levels of assertiveness, self-confidence, trustworthiness, dependability, and ability to control stress. Their Scholastic Aptitude Test (SAT) scores were 210 points higher than the "instant gratification" group!

The ones who had rung the bell quickly seemed more likely to have behavioural problems, both in school and at home, they got lower SAT scores, they struggled in stressful situations, often had trouble paying attention and found it difficult to maintain friendships.

He then did a further study to track them into their

late thirties. The low delayers had a significantly higher body-mass index and were more likely to have had problems with drugs.

Many psychologists had concluded that raw intelligence was the most important variable when it comes to predicting success in life. Mischel, however, argues that intelligence is largely at the mercy of self control. "What we are really measuring with the marshmallow test isn't willpower or self control," he argues. "It's much more important than that. This task forces kids to find a way to make the situation work for them. They want the second marshmallow, but how can they get it? We can't control the world, but we can control how we think about it."

You might wonder about Mischel's own children. Carolyn is now an associate psychology professor at the University of Puget Sound. Craig, meanwhile, moved to Los Angeles and has spent his career doing "All kinds of things" in the entertainment industry, mostly in production. "Sure, I wish I had been a more patient person," Craig says. "Looking back, there are definitely moments when it would have helped me make better career choices and stuff."

APPENDIX

The NASA Space pen

Here is a story which could easily be an urban myth. In fact it is not only true but justified by science. I include the short story, and also the explanation.

> "During the height of the space race in the 1960s, legend has it, NASA was faced with a major problem. Their scientists realised that pens could not function in the vacuum of space. The astronauts needed a way to write things down.

> "They spent years and 1.5 million taxpayer dollars to develop a pen that could put ink to paper without gravity. It enjoyed minor success on the commercial market.

> "The Russians were faced with the same problem. They simply handed their cosmonauts pencils."

This tale with its message of simplicity and thrift is often used as an example of a failure of common sense in a bureaucracy. However, there were good reasons for the development of the anti-gravity space pen, and taxpayer dollars were not used.

Originally, NASA astronauts, like the Soviet cosmonauts, used pencils. In fact, NASA ordered 34 mechanical pencils from Houston's Tycam Engineering Manufacturing, Inc., in 1965. They paid $4,382.50 or $128.89 per pencil. When these prices became public, there was an outcry and NASA scrambled to find something cheaper for the astronauts to use.

In fact, pencils would not have been the best choice anyway. The tips flaked and broke off, drifting in microgravity where they could potentially harm an astronaut or equipment. And pencils are flammable — a quality NASA wanted to avoid in onboard objects after the Apollo 1 fire.

The Fisher Pen Company, reportedly invested $1 million to create what is now commonly known as the space pen. None of this investment money came from NASA's coffers — the agency only became involved after the pen was dreamed into existence. In 1965 Fisher patented a pen that could write upside-down, in frigid or roasting conditions (down to minus 50 degrees Fahrenheit or up to 400 degrees F), and even underwater or in other liquids. If too hot, though, the ink turned green instead of its normal blue.

That same year, Fisher offered the AG-7 "Anti-Gravity" Space Pen to NASA. Because of the earlier mechanical pencil fiasco, NASA was hesitant. But, after testing the space pen intensively, the agency decided to use it on spaceflights beginning in 1967.

Unlike most ballpoint pens, Fisher's pen does not rely on gravity to get the ink flowing. The cartridge is instead pressurised with nitrogen at 35 pounds per square inch. This pressure pushes the ink toward the tungsten carbide ball at the pen's tip.

The ink, too, differs from that of other pens. Fisher used ink that stays a gel-like solid until the movement of the ballpoint turns it into a fluid. The pressurised nitrogen also prevents air from mixing with the ink so it cannot evaporate or oxidise.

According to an Associated Press report from February 1968, NASA ordered 400 of Fisher's antigravity ballpoint pens for the Apollo program. A year later, the Soviet Union ordered 100 pens and 1,000 ink cartridges to use on their Soyuz space missions. The AP later noted that both NASA and the Soviet space agency received the same 40 percent discount for buying their pens in bulk. They both paid $2.39 per pen instead of $3.98.

The space pen also played a part in the Apollo 11 disaster. According to the Fisher Space Pen Company, the astronauts also used the pen to fix a broken arming switch, enabling their return to Earth.

Since the late 1960s American astronauts and Russian cosmonauts have used Fisher's pens. In fact, Fisher has created a whole line of space pens. A newer pen, called the Shuttle Pen, was used on NASA's space shuttles and on the Russian space station, Mir.

The Strangest Secret

This is a famous story by Earl Nightingale

"I'd like you tell you about the strangest secret in the world", said Nightingale in one of his recordings.

Some years ago, the late Nobel prize-winning Dr. Albert Schweitzer was being interviewed in London and the reporter asked him, "Doctor, what's wrong with men today?" The great doctor was silent a moment, and then he said, "Men simply don't think."

It's about this that I want to talk with you. We live today in a golden age. This is an era that man has looked forward to, dreamed of and worked toward for thousands of years. But since it's here, we pretty well take it for granted. We in America are particularly fortunate to live in the richest land that ever existed on the face of the earth, a land of abundant opportunity for everyone. But, do you know what happens?

Let's take 100 men who start even at the age of 25. Do you have any idea what will happen to those men by the time they are 65? These 100 men who all start even at the age of 25 believe they're going to be successful. If you asked any one of these men if he wanted to be a success, he'd tell you that he did, and you'd notice that he was eager toward life; that there was a certain sparkle to his eye, an erectness to his carriage, and life seemed like a pretty interesting adventure to him. But by the time they're 65, one will be rich. Four will be financially independent, five will still be working, 54 will be broke.

Now, think a moment. Out of the 100, only five make the grade. Why do so many fail? What has happened to the sparkle that was there when they were 25? What's become of the dreams, the hopes, the plans? And why is there such a large disparity between what these men intended to do, and what they actually accomplished?

When we say about 5% achieve success, we have to define success. And here's the definition I've ever been able to find: Success is the progressive realisation of a worthy ideal. If a man is working toward a pre-determined goal and knows where he's going, that man is a success. If he's not doing that, he's a failure. Success is the progressive realisation of a worthy ideal.

Rolo May, the distinguished psychiatrist wrote a wonderful book called "Man's Search for Himself." In this book, he shows the opposite of courage in our society is not cowardice. It is conformity.

And there you have the trouble today. It's conformity – people acting like everyone else without knowing why, without knowing where they're going.

Think of it. In America right now, there are over 18 million people 65 years of age and older, and most of them are broke. They're dependent on someone else for life's necessities.

We learn to read by the time we're seven. We learn to make a living by the time we're 25. Usually, by that time, now that we're making a living we're supporting a family. And yet, by the time we're 65, we haven't learned how to become financially independent in the richest land that has ever been known.

Why? We conform. The trouble is that we're acting like the wrong percentage group – the 95 who don't succeed.

Why do these people conform? Well, they really

don't know. These people believed that their lives are shaped by circumstances, by things that happen to them by exterior forces, they're outer-directed people. They are outer-directed people.

A survey was made one time that covered a lot of men, working men, and these men were asked, "Why do you work?" "Why do you get up in the morning?" 19 out of 20 had no idea.

If you ask them they will say, "Well, everyone goes to work in the morning," and that's the reason they do it – because everyone else is doing it.

Now, let's get back to our definition of success. Who succeeds?

The only person who succeeds is the person who is progressively realising a worthy ideal. It is the person who says, "I am going to become this," and then begins to work towards that goal.

I'll tell you who the successful people are. A success is the school teacher who is teaching school because that's what he or she wants to do. A success is the woman who is a wife and mother because she wanted to become a wife and mother and is doing a good job of it. A success is the man who runs the corner gas station because that was his dream. That's what he wanted to do.

A success is the successful salesman who wants to become a top-notch salesman and grow and build within his organisation. A success is anyone who is doing deliberately a pre-determined job because that's what he decided to do deliberately. But only 1 out of 20 does that.

That's why today there isn't really any competition unless we make it for ourselves. Instead of competing, all we have to do is create. For 20 years, I looked for the key which would determine what would happen to a human being.

Was there a key, I wanted to know, which would make the future a promise that we could foretell to a large extent. Was there a key that would guarantee a person's becoming successful if he only knew about it and knew how to use it?

Well, there is such a key. And I found it.

Have you ever wondered why so many men work so hard and honestly without ever achieving anything in particular, and others don't seem to work hard and yet seem to get everything? They seem to have a magic touch.

You've heard them say that about someone. "Everything he touches turns to gold." Have you ever noticed that a man who becomes successful tends to continue to become successful?

On the other hand, have you noticed how a man who's a failure tends to continue to fail? Well, it's because of goals. Some of us have goals; some don't. People with goals succeed because they know where they're going. It's that simple.

Think of a ship leaving a harbour and think of it with a complete voyage mapped out and planned. The captain and crew know exactly where it's going and how long it will take. It has a definite goal. 9,999 times out of 10,000 it will get to where it started out to get.

Now let's take another ship, just like the first, only let's not put a crew on it, or a captain at the helm. Let's give it no aiming point, no goal, and no destination. We just start the engines and let it go.

I think you'll agree with me that if it gets out of the harbour at all, it will either sink or wind up on some deserted beach, a derelict. It can't go any place because it has no destination and no guidance.

It's the same with a human being. Take the salesman for example. There is no other person in the world today with the future of a good salesman. Selling is the world's highest paid profession, if we're good at it and if we know where we're going.

Every company needs top-notch salesmen, and they reward those men. The sky is the limit for them. But how many can you find?

Someone once said the human race is fixed. Not to prevent the strong from winning, but to prevent the weak from losing.

The American economy today can be likened to a convoy in time of war. The entire economy is slowed down to protect its weakest link, just as the convoy had to go at the speed that will permit its slowest vessel to remain in formation.

That's why it's so easy to make a living today. It takes no particular brains or talent to make a living and support a family. We have a plateau on so-called security, if that's what person is looking for. But we do have to decide how high above this plateau we want to aim.

Now let's get back to the Strangest Secret in the World, the story I wanted to tell you today.

Why do men with goals succeed in life, and men without them fail? Well, let me tell you something which, if you really understand it, will alter your life immediately. If you understand completely what I'm going to tell you from this moment on, your life will never be the same again.

You will suddenly find that good luck just seems to be attracted to you, the things you want just seem to fall in line, and from now on you won't have the problems, the worries, the gnawing lump of anxiety that perhaps you've experienced before. Doubt and fear will now be things of the past.

Throughout history, the great wise men and teachers, philosophers, and prophets have disagreed with one another on many different things. It's only on this one point that they are in complete and unanimous agreement.

Listen to what Marcus Aurelius, the great Roman

Emperor said: "A man's life is what his thoughts make of it."

Disraeli said this: "Everything comes if a man will only wait. I've brought myself by long meditation to the conviction that a human being with a settled purpose must accomplish it, and nothing can resist a will that will stake even existence for its fulfillment."

Ralph Waldo Emerson said this: "A man is what he thinks about all day long."

William James said, "The greatest discovery of my generation is that human beings can alter their lives by altering their attitudes of mind."

And he also said, "We need only in cold blood act as if the thing in question were real, and it will become infallibly real by growing into such a connection with our life that it will become real. It will become so knit with habit and emotion that our interests in it will be those which characterize belief."

He also said, "If you only care enough for a result, you will almost certainly obtain it. If you wish to be rich, you will be rich. If you wish to be learned, you will be learned. If you wish to be good, you will be good. Only you must, then, really wish these things, and wish them exclusively, and not wish at the same time a hundred other incompatible things just as strongly."

In the Bible you will read in Mark 9-23: "If thou canst believe, all things are possible to him that believeth."

My old friend Dr. Norman Vincent Peale put it this way: "This is one of the greatest laws in the universe. Fervently do I wish I had discovered it as a very young man. It dawned upon me much later in life, and I found it to be the greatest discovery, if not my greatest discovery, outside my relationship to God. The great law briefly and simply stated is if you think in negative terms, you will get negative results. If you think in positive terms, you will achieve positive results."

"That is the simple fact," he went on to say, "Which is of the basis of an astonishing law of prosperity and success. In three words: Believe and Succeed."

William Shakespeare put it this way: "Our doubts are traitors and make us lose the good we oft might win by fearing to attempt."

George Bernard Shaw said: "People are always blaming their circumstances for what they are. I don't believe in circumstances. The people who get on in this world are the people who get up and look for the circumstances they want, and if they can't find them, make them."

Well, it's pretty apparent, isn't it? And every person who discovered this, for a while, believed that they were the first to work it out. We become what we think about.

It stands to reason that a person who is thinking about a concrete and worthwhile goal is going to reach it, because that's what he's thinking about. And we become what we think about.

Conversely, the man who has no goal, who doesn't know where they are going, and whose thoughts must therefore be thoughts of confusion, anxiety, fear, and worry becomes what they think about. His life becomes one of frustration, fear, anxiety, and worry. And if he thinks about nothing, he becomes nothing.

Now how does it work? Why do we become what we think about?

Well, I'll tell you how it works as far as we know. To do this, I want to talk about a situation that parallels the human mind.

Suppose a farmer has some land and it's good, fertile land. Now, the land gives the farmer a choice. He may plant in that land whatever he chooses. The land doesn't care. It's up to the farmer to make the decision.

Remember, we're comparing the human mind with the land because, the mind, like the land, doesn't care what you plant in it. It will return what you plant, but it doesn't care what you plant.

Now let's say that the farmer has two seeds in his hand – one a seed of corn; the other is nightshade, a deadly poison. He digs two little holes in the earth and he plants both seeds; one corn, the other nightshade. He covers up the holes, waters, and takes care of the land.

What will happen? Invariably, the land will return what's planted. As it's written in the Bible, "As ye sow, so shall ye reap."

Remember, the land doesn't care. It will return poison in just as wonderful abundance as it will corn. So up come the two plants – one corn, one poison.

The human mind is far more fertile, far more incredible and mysterious than the land, but it works the same way. It doesn't care what we plant – success, failure. A concrete, worthwhile goal or confusion, misunderstanding, fear, anxiety, and so on. But what we plant, it must return to us.

You see, the human mind is the last great unexplored continent on earth. It contains riches beyond our wildest dreams. It will return anything we want to plant. So you may say, if that is true, why don't people use their minds more?

Well, I think they've figured out an answer to that one too. Our mind comes as standard equipment at birth. It's free. And things that are given to us for nothing, we place little value on. Things that we pay money for, we value.

The paradox is that exactly the reverse is true. Everything that's really worthwhile in life came to us free: our minds, our souls, our bodies, our hopes, our dreams, our ambitions, our intelligence, our love of family and children and friends and country. All these priceless possessions are free.

But the things that cost us money are actually very

cheap and can be replaced at any time. A good man can be completely wiped out and make another fortune. He can do that several times. Even if our home burns down, we can rebuild it. But the things we got for nothing, we can never replace.

The human mind is not used because we take it for granted. Familiarity breeds contempt. It can do any kind of job we assign to it, but generally speaking, we use it for little jobs instead of big important ones. Universities have proved that most of us are operating on about ten percent or less of our abilities.

So decide now. What is it you want? Plant your goal in your mind. It's the most important decision you'll ever make in your entire life.

What is it you want? Do you want to be an outstanding salesman, a better worker at your particular job?

Do you want to go places in your company, in your community? Do you want to get rich?

All you have got to do is plant that seed in your mind, care for it, work steadily towards your goal, and it will become a reality. It not only will, there's no way that it cannot.

You see, that's a law, like the laws of Sir Isaac Newton, the laws of gravity. If you get on top of a building and jump off, you'll always go down. You'll never go up.

And it's the same with all the other laws of nature. They always work. They're inflexible.

Think about your goal in a relaxed, positive way. Picture yourself in your mind's eye as having already achieved this goal. See yourself doing the things you will be doing when you have reached your goal.

Ours has been called a Phenobarbitol Age, the age of ulcers and nervous breakdowns and tranquilizers. At a time when medical research has raised us to a new plateau of good health and longevity, far too many of us worry ourselves into an early grave trying to cope with things in our own little personal ways, without learning a few great laws that will take care of everything for us.

These things we bring on ourselves through our habitual way of thinking. Every one of us is the sum total of our own thoughts. He is where he is because that's exactly where we really want or feel we deserve to be, whether we'll admit that or not.

Each of us must live off the fruit of his thoughts in the future, because what you think today and tomorrow, next month and next year, will mold your life and determine your future. You're guided by your mind.

I remember one time I was driving through eastern Arizona and I saw one of those giant earth-moving machines roaring along the road at about 35 miles an hour with what looked like 30 tons of dirt in it – a tremendous, incredible machine – and there was a little man perched way up on top with the wheel in his hands, guiding it.

As I drove along, I was struck by the similarity of that machine with the human mind. Just suppose you are sitting at the controls of such a vast source of energy. Are you going to sit back and fold your arms and let it run itself into a ditch or are you going to keep both hands firmly on the wheel and control and direct this power to a specific, worthwhile purpose?

It's up to you. You're in the driver's seat.

You see, the very law that gives us success is a two-edged sword. We must control our thinking. The same rule that can lead a man to a life of success, wealth, happiness, and all the things they ever dreamed of for themselves and his family, that very same law can lead them into the gutter. It's all in how he uses it – for good or for bad.

This is The Strangest Secret in the world. Why do I say it's strange, and why do I call it a secret?

Actually, it isn't a secret at all. It was first promulgated by some of the earliest wise men, and it appears again and again throughout the Bible. But very few people have learned it or understand it. That's why it's strange, and why for some equally strange reason it virtually remains a secret.

I believe you could go out and walk down the main street of your town and ask one person after another what the secret of success is and you probably wouldn't run into one person in a month that could tell you.

This information is enormously valuable to us if we really understand it and apply it. It's valuable to us not only for our own lives, but the lives of those around us, our families, employees, associates, and friends.

Life should be an exciting adventure. It should never be a bore. A man should work fully, be alive. He should be glad to get out of bed in the morning. He should be doing a job he likes to do because he does it well.

One time I heard Grove Patterson, the great late editor-in-chief of the Toledo Daily Blade make a speech and as he concluded his speech he said something I've never forgotten. He said, "My years in the newspaper business have convinced me of several things. Among them, that people are basically good, and that we came from someplace and we are going someplace. So we should make our time here an exciting adventure. The architect of the universe didn't build a stairway leading nowhere. The greatest teacher of all, the carpenter from the Plains of Galilee of all gave us the secret time and time again: As ye believe, so shall it be done – unto you."

Brefi Group

Vision

Brefi Group believes in a world of work that enables individuals and teams to achieve their potential in a congruent and ethical manner.

Mission statement

"Brefi Group helps individuals and teams in organisations discover and achieve their potential so that they can become more effective with less stress."

Values

Underpinning beliefs: -

- Each and every individual and organisation has the potential to achieve more.

- As individuals and organisations are aligned and discover their potential, corporate performance improves.

- As individuals are aligned and discover their potential, they impact positively on the wider society.

We value: –

- Learning and development. We role model learning and behave as co-learners when working with clients. We are committed to our own personal and professional development.

- The practice and maintenance of high ethical and professional standards.

- The individual's knowledge of their own business and available resources.

- The bottom-line impact of personal and professional development

- The well being and performance of individuals at work, both separately and as members of teams.

www.brefigroup.co.uk